THE BOOK OF

WINE

THE BOOK OF
WINE

STUART WALTON

SMITHMARK

This edition published in 1997
by SMITHMARK Publishers, a division of US Media Holdings, Inc.
16 East 32nd Street
New York
NY 10016
USA

SMITHMARK books are available for bulk purchase for sales and promotion and
premium use. For details write or call the manager of special sales,
SMITHMARK Publishers, 16 East 32nd Street, New York, NY 10016
(212) 532-6600

© 1997 Anness Publishing Limited
Produced by Anness Publishing Limited
Hermes House
88-89 Blackfriars Road
London SE1 8HA

ISBN 0 7651 9422 8

Publisher: Joanna Lorenz
Senior Editor: Linda Fraser
Copy Editor: Jane Hughes
Designer: Sheila Volpe
Picture Researcher: Lynda Marshall
Special photography and styling: Steve Baxter with Roisin Neild pp. 6-7, 10, 11, 12,
13, 14, 15, 16, 17, 18, 19, 20, 21, 22-3
Illustrator: Madeleine David

Photographs: With the exception of sources noted, all photographic
material supplied by Cephas Picture Library:
Bridgeman Art Library p.8 Courtesy Pushkin Museum, Moscow, p.9 Courtesy British
Library, London, James Hawes p.41 (right), Patrick Eager p.51
Cover: Cephas Picture Library, Steve Baxter

Printed in Singapore by Star Standard Industries Pte. Ltd.

1 3 5 7 9 10 8 6 4 2

Note: All opinions expressed in this book are those of the author.

CONTENTS

INTRODUCTION

Van Gogh's depiction of grape-harvesting at Arles in the 1880s (above) would still be recognisable today in parts of southern France.

At the heart of the enormous boom in wine consumption that has taken place in the English-speaking world over the last two decades or so is a fascinating, happy paradox.

In the days when wine was exclusively the preserve of a narrow cultural elite, bought either at auction or from gentleman wine merchants in wing collars and bow-ties, to be stored in rambling cellars and decanted to order by one's butler, the ordinary drinker didn't get a look-in. Wine was considered a highly technical subject, in which anybody without the necessary ability could only fall flat on his or her face in embarrassment. It wasn't just that you needed a refined aesthetic sensibility for the stuff if it wasn't to be hopelessly wasted on you. It required an intimate knowledge of what came from where, and what it was supposed to taste like.

Those were times, however, when wine appreciation essentially meant a familiarity with the great French classics, with perhaps a little sweet wine from Germany and a smattering of the traditional fortified wines - sherry, port and madeira. That was what the wine trade dealt in. These days, wine is bought daily in supermarkets and high-street chains to be consumed that evening, hardly anybody has a cellar to store it in and most don't even possess a decanter. Above all, the wines of literally

dozens of countries are available on our market. When a supermarket offers its customers a couple of fruity little numbers from Brazil, we scarcely raise an eyebrow.

It seems, in other words, that the commercial jungle that wine has now become has not in the slightest deterred people from plunging adventurously into the thickets in order to taste and see. Consumers are no longer intimidated by the thought of needing to know their Pouilly-Fumé from their Pouilly-Fuissé, their Bardolino from their Brunello, just at the very moment when there is more to know than ever before.

The reason for this new mood of confidence is not hard to find. It is on virtually every wine label from Australia, America, New Zealand, South Africa and South America: the name of the grape from which the wine is made. At one time, that might have sounded like a fairly technical approach in itself. Why should native English-speakers need to know what Cabernet Sauvignon, Chardonnay or Sauvignon Blanc were? The answer lies in the popularity that wines made from those grape varieties now enjoy. Consumers recognise them as brand names effectively, and have acquired a basic lexicon of wine that can serve them even when confronted with those Brazilian upstarts.

In the wine heartlands of Europe, especially France, they are scared to death of that trend – not because they think their wine isn't as good as the best from California or South Australia (what French winemaker will ever admit that?) but because they don't traditionally call their wines Cabernet Sauvignon or Chardonnay. They call them Château Ducru-Beaucaillou or Corton-Charlemagne, and they aren't about to change. Some areas, notably the large swathes of the Midi in the middle of southern France, have now produced a generation of growers (not all of them French) using the varietal names on their labels and are tempting consumers back to French wine. It will be an uphill struggle, but there is probably no other way if France is to avoid simply becoming a speciality source of old-fashioned wines for old-fashioned connoisseurs.

Wine consumption was also given a significant boost in the early 1990s by the pioneering work of Dr Serge Renaud, a nutritionist based at Lyon, who has spent many years investigating the reasons for the uncannily low incidence of coronary heart disease in the south of France. One of the major findings to have emerged from his studies is that the fat-derived cholesterol that builds up in the arteries and can eventually lead to heart trouble by blocking the heart's supply of oxygen can be dispersed by the tannins in wine. Tannin is derived from the skins of grapes, and is therefore present in higher levels in red wines, because they have to be infused with their skins to attain their colour. The truth was out: wine is good for you.

That news caused a huge upsurge in red wine consumption in the United States when a television documentary about Dr Renaud's findings was aired. It has not generally been accorded the prominence it deserves in the UK, largely because the medical profession still sees all alcohol as a menace to health, and is constantly calling for it to be made prohibitively expensive. Certainly, the manufacturers of anticoagulant drugs might have something to lose if we all got the message that we would do just as well by our hearts, and be considerably happier, by taking half a bottle of red wine every day.

Wine is there to be enjoyed, and there has never been so much good wine about as there is today. This book is designed to help you get your bearings a little when it comes to storing and serving wine and with some of the more commonly encountered grape varieties. It is not an academic textbook loaded with technicalities but is aimed squarely at those who already enjoy drinking wine and would like to deepen their knowledge of where it is made and what goes into it.

The first part of the book deals with keeping, serving and tasting wine. There is advice on professional tasting technique and a guide to analysing the elements that make up a wine's aroma and flavour characteristics. Next comes information on where to keep wine, what to open it with, whether to let it breathe or not and how to decant those wines that need it. A comparative look at different types of wine glass is followed by a general guide to matching wine and food. A final section gives pointers to the types of information presented on wine labels.

The second part takes a look at twelve of the most important grape varieties used in international winemaking. I have tried to give an indication of the different regional styles each grape takes on, how the wines typically taste, and also an overview of what debates are currently taking place among wine professionals with regard to some of them, so that you can make up your own mind where you stand and not have somebody else's opinion foisted on you.

Wine possesses a virtually limitless ability to surprise. No two wines are alike; some say no two bottles are alike. It all depends on the context, the company, the bottle and you. I hope you enjoy reading about it, but even more, I hope you will go on to find ever greater pleasure in the wines that await you. That is what this book is all about.

The vintage has traditionally been one of the ceremonial high points of the year in Europe's wine-growing regions, as this illustration from the medieval Book of Hours, c.1520 (above) vividly demonstrates.

Stuart Walton

PRINCIPLES *of* TASTING

All that sniffing, swirling and spitting that the professional winetasters engage in is more than just a way of showing off; it really can immeasurably enhance the appreciation of any wine.

THE WINETASTER'S ritual of peering into a glass, swirling it around and sniffing suspiciously at it, before taking a mouthful only to spit it out again looks like a highly mysterious and technical procedure to the uninitiated. It is, however, a sequence of perfectly logical steps that can immeasurably enhance the enjoyment of good wine. Once learned, they become almost second nature to even the novice taster.

Don't pour a full glass for tasting because you're going to need room for swirling, but allow a little more than the wine waiter in a restaurant tends to offer. About a third full is the optimum amount.

When pouring a tasting sample, be sure to leave enough room in the glass for giving it a good swirl (below).

Firstly, have a good look at the wine by holding it up to the daylight or other light source. Is it clear or cloudy? Does it contain sediment or other solid matter? In the case of red wines, tilt the glass away from you against a white surface and look at the colour of the liquid at the far edge. Older wines start to fade at the rim, the deep red taking on an autumnal brownish or tawny hue.

Now swirl the glass gently. The point of this is to activate the aromatic compounds in the wine, so that when you come to stick your nose in, the bouquet can be fully appreciated. Swirling takes a bit of practice (start with a glass of water over the kitchen sink) but the aim is to get a fairly vigorous wave circulating in the liquid. If you are nervous about performing the swirl in mid-air, there is nothing wrong with doing it while the glass is still on the table and then bringing it to your nose, but beware of scraping your best crystal around on a rough wooden tabletop.

When sniffing, tilt the glass towards your face and get your nose slightly inside it, keeping it within the lower half of the opening of the glass. The head should be bent forward a little with the glass tipped at a 45° angle to meet it. Inhale gently (as if you were sniffing a flower, not filling your lungs on a blustery clifftop) and for a good three or four seconds. The scents a wine offers may change during the course of one sniff. Nosing a wine can reveal a great deal about its origins and the way it was made, but don't overdo it. The sense of smell is quickly neutralised. Two or three sniffs should tell you as much as you need to know.

Now comes the tricky part. The reason that wine experts pull those ridiculous faces when they take a mouthful is that they are trying to spread the wine around all the different taste-sensitive parts of the tongue. At its very tip are the receptors for sweetness. Just a little back from those, saltiness is registered. Acidity or sourness is tasted on the sides of the tongue, while bitterness is sensed at the very back. So roll the wine around your mouth as thoroughly as you can.

It helps to maximise the flavour of a wine if you take in air while it's in your mouth. To reduce the risk of dribbling, make sure the head is now back in an upright position. Using gentle suction with the lips pursed, draw in some breath. It will only be necessary to allow the tiniest opening - less than the width of a pencil - and to suck in immediately. Again, practise over the sink. Close the lips again, and breathe downwards through the nose. In this way, the taste of the wine is transmitted through the nasal passages as well as via the tongue, and the whole sensation is more intense. And *think* about the taste. What messages is the wine giving you? Do you like it or not?

When you have tasted the mouthful of wine, you can either swallow it - much the best thing in polite company - or, if you are tasting a number of wines at a time of day when you wouldn't normally be drinking, then spit it out. At public tastings, there will be buckets or lined boxes for spitting into, or else at an outdoor fair or in a marquee at a wine show, spit it out on the ground, taking care not to spray the shoes of unsuspecting passers-by. Spit confidently, with the tongue behind the ejected liquid, so as to avoid it trickling down your chin, but spit downwards. You are not aiming to extinguish a fire.

There are five principal elements to look for in the taste of a wine. Learn to concentrate on each one individually while tasting, and you will start to put together a set of analytical tools with which to evaluate the quality of any wine.

Dryness/Sweetness From bone-dry Chablis at one end of the spectrum to the most luscious Liqueur Muscats at the other, through a broad range of intermediary styles, the amount of natural sugar a wine contains is perhaps its most easily noted attribute.

Acidity There are many different types of acid in wine, the most important being tartaric, which is present in unfermented grape juice. How sharp does the wine feel at the edges of the tongue? Good acidity is necessary to contribute a feeling of freshness to a young wine, and to help the best wines to age. In a poor vintage though, when the grapes didn't ripen properly, an excessive sourness or even bitterness can spoil a wine. Don't confuse dryness with acidity. A very dry wine like fino sherry can actually be quite low in acid, while the sweetest Sauternes will contain sufficient acidity to offset its sugar.

Tannin Tannin is present in the stalks and pips of fresh grapes, but also in the skins. Since the colour in red wine comes from the skins (the juice of even black grapes being colourless), some tannin is inevitably extracted along with it. In the mouth, it gives that furry, drying feeling that makes very young reds hard to drink, but it disappears gradually as they mature in the bottle.

Oak Many wines are matured in oak barrels, and may even have gone through their initial fermentation in oak, and the flavour imparted to them by contact with the wood is an easy one to appreciate, particularly in the case of whites. An aroma or taste of vanilla or other sweet spice such as nutmeg or cinnamon is a strong indicator of the presence of oak, as is an overall feeling of creamy smoothness on the palate in the case of the richer reds. If the barrels a wine was kept in were heavily charred (or "toasted") on the insides, the wine will display a pronounced smokiness like toast left under the grill a little too long or a match that has just been blown out.

Fruit Anybody who has read a newspaper or magazine wine column in which the writer describes wines as tasting of raspberries, passion fruit, melon and glacé cherries (often all at once) will have wondered if there isn't an element of kiddology in it all. In fact, there are sound biochemical reasons for the resemblance of wines to the flavours of other foods (and not just fruit, but vegetables, herbs and spices too). In the sections on the main grape varieties, I have suggested some of the flavours most commonly met with in the wines made from those grapes. Let your imagination run free when tasting. Bright fruit flavours are among the most charming features a wine can possess.

A gentle swirling action of the hand is sufficient to produce quite a vigorous wave in the glass (above).

Sniff lightly and long, with the nose slightly below the rim of the glass (above).

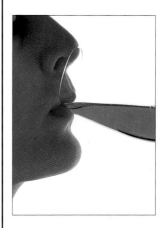

Take a good mouthful of the wine, in order to coat all surfaces of the mouth with it (above).

STORING *and* SERVING

Where is the best place to keep wine for maturation? Should it be allowed to breathe before being served? What does decanting an old wine involve? None of these questions is as technical as it seems.

NONE OF THE TECHNICALITIES involved in the storage and serving of wine needs to be too complicated. The following guidelines are aimed at keeping things simple.

Creating a cellar Starting a wine collection requires a certain amount of ingenuity now that most of us live in flats or houses without cellars. If you have bought a large parcel of wine that you don't want to touch for years, you can pay a nominal fee to a wine merchant to cellar it for you, but the chances are that you may only have a couple of dozen bottles at any one time. Where to keep it?

The two main points to bear in mind are that bottles should be stored horizontally and away from sources of heat. You can pile them on top of each other if they are all the same shape, but it's safer and more convenient to invest in a simple wooden or plastic wine rack. Keeping the bottles on their sides means the wine is in constant contact with the corks, preventing them from drying out and imparting off-flavours to the wine.

Don't put your bottles in the cupboard next to the storage heater or near the cooker because heat is a menace to wine. Equally, don't leave it

A simple winerack is much the best way of storing bottles (right). This one allows enough space to see the labels too, so that they don't have to be pulled out to identify them.

in the garden shed in sub-zero temperatures. Choose a cool cupboard that's not too high up (remember that heat rises) and where it can rest in peace in the dark.

Serving temperatures The conventional wisdom that white wine should be served chilled and red wine at room temperature is essentially correct, but it isn't the whole story.

Don't over-chill white wine or its flavours will be muted. Light, acidic whites, sparkling wines and very sweet wines (and rosés too for that matter) should be served at no higher than about 10°C (50°F) but the best Chardonnays, dry Semillons and Alsace wines can afford to be a little less cool than that.

Reds, on the other hand, generally benefit from being slightly cooler than the ambient temperature in a well-heated home. Never warm the bottle by a radiator as that will make the wine taste muddy. Some lighter, fruity reds such

as young Beaujolais, Dolcetto or the lighter Loire or New Zealand reds are best served lightly chilled - about an hour in the refrigerator.

Breathing Should red wine be allowed to breathe? In the case of matured reds that are intended to be drunk on release, like Rioja Reservas or the softer, barrel-aged Cabernet Sauvignons of Australia, the answer is that there is probably no point. Young reds with some tannin, or immature hard acidity, do round out with a bit of air contact, though. Either pour the wine into a decanter or jug half an hour or so before serving or, if you haven't anything suitable for the table, pour it into another container and then funnel it back into the bottle. Simply drawing the cork won't in itself make any difference because only the wine in the neck is in contact with the air. And remember the wine will develop in any case in the glass as you slowly sip it.

Here is an ingeniously designed winerack that ensures that the undersides of the corks are kept constantly in contact with the wine, thus preventing them from drying out.

Corkscrews The spin-handled corkscrew is undoubtedly the easiest to use because it involves one continuous motion and very little effort. The type with side-levers is less good because it often needs two or three attempts with longer corks. If you are good at displays of brute force, the Wine Waiter's Friend is the model for you, but a particularly obstinate cork can make you look very silly. In theory, the object is to insert the corkscrew far enough into the cork to be able to draw it without piercing the underside and risking fragments of cork falling into the wine. A bartender once taught me a trick for removing bits of cork before pouring. It involved giving the bottle one sharp flick in the general direction of the sink. If your aim is accurate, try it. It wastes less wine than pouring it, cork lumps and all, into a glass and then discarding it.

Some corkscrews are equipped with a foil cutter (above), allowing you to remove a neat circle from the top of the capsule for uncorking.

The most basic type of corkscrew (top left) involves simple tugging; it is far easier to use the opener (bottom left) as it requires hardly any effort; the levered model (top right) isn't bad, but can break a large cork. The very chic Fish corkscrew (bottom right) works with a gentle spring action.

Opening fizz Many people are still intimidated about opening sparkling wines. Remember that the longer a bottle of fizz has been able to rest before opening, the less lively it will be. If it has been very badly shaken up, it may need a week or more to settle. Also, the colder it is, the less likely it will be to go off like a firecracker.

Once the foil has been removed and the wire cage untwisted and taken off too, grasp the cork firmly and take hold of the lower half of the bottle. The advice generally given is to turn the bottle rather than the cork, but in practice most people probably do both (twisting in opposite directions, of course). Work very gently and, when you feel or see the cork beginning to rise, control it every millimetre of the way with your thumb over the top. It should be possible then to ease it out without it popping. If the wine does spurt, put a finger in the neck, but don't completely stopper it again.

When pouring, fill each glass to just under half-full, and then go round again to top them up once the initial fizz has subsided. Pour fairly slowly so that the wine doesn't foam over the sides. Do not pour into tilted glasses: you aren't serving lager.

Decanting Decanting can help to make a tough young wine a bit more supple, but it is only absolutely necessary if the wine being served is heavily sedimented. In that case, stand the bottle upright for the best part of the day you intend to serve it (from the night before is even better) so that the deposits settle to the bottom. After uncorking, pour the wine in a slow but continuous stream into the decanter, looking into the neck of the bottle. When the sediment starts working its way into the neck as you reach the end, stop pouring. The amount of wine you are left with should be negligible enough to throw away, but if there's more than half a glass, then strain the remainder through a clean muslin cloth. Do *not* use coffee filter-papers or tissue as they will alter the flavour of the wine.

When opening sparkling wines, it is important to restrain the release of the cork (left). Control it every millimetre of the way once it begins to push out.

The quicker you pour, the more vigorous will be the foaming of the wine in the glass (left). Pour carefully to avoid any wastage through overflowing.

The Champagne Saver is a good way of preserving the fizz in any unfinished bottles of sparkling wine (left). Some swear, quite unscientifically, by inserting a spoon-handle in the neck.

GLASSES

Wine doesn't have to be served in the most expensive glassware to show it to advantage, but there are a few basic principles to bear in mind when choosing glasses that will help you get the best from your bottle.

Glasses these days come in all shapes and sizes (below). From left to right in the foreground are: a good red or white wine glass; a technically correct champagne flute; the famous "Paris goblet" much beloved of wine-bars, not a bad shape but too small; an elegant-looking but inefficient sparkling wine glass with flared opening, causing greater dispersal of bubbles; a sherry copita, also useful for other fortified wines.

ALTHOUGH I CAN scarcely remember any champagne that tasted better than the stuff we poured into polystyrene cups huddled in my student quarters after the examination results went up, the truth is that, certainly when you're in the mood to concentrate, it does make a difference what you drink wine from. Not only the appearance but the smell and, yes, even the taste of a wine can be substantially enhanced by using the proper glasses.

They don't have to be prohibitively costly, although - as with everything else - the best doesn't come cheap. The celebrated Austrian glassmaker Georg Riedel has taken the science of wineglasses to its ultimate degree, working out what specific aromatic and flavour components in each type of wine need emphasising, and designing his glasses accordingly. Some of

them are very peculiar shapes indeed, but they undeniably do the trick.

There are some broad guidelines that we can all follow, however, when choosing glasses. Firstly, always choose a plain glass to set off your best wines. Coloured ones, or even those that have just the stems and bases tinted, can distort the appearance of white wines particularly. And, although cut crystal can look very beautiful, I tend to avoid it for wines because it doesn't make for the clearest view of the liquid in the glass.

Look for a deep, wide bowl that tapers significantly towards the mouth. With glasses like that, the aromatic compounds in the wine can be released more generously, both because the deeper bowl allows for a more demonstrative swirling action than anything too small, and because the narrower opening channels the

scents of the wine to your nostrils more efficiently. A flared opening disperses much of the bouquet to the surrounding air.

Traditionally, red wine is served in bigger glasses than white. If you are serving both colours at a grand gastronomic evening, it helps to allot different wines their particular glasses, but the assumption is that reds, especially mature wines, need more space in which to breathe. More development of the wine will take place in the glass than in any decanter or jug the wine may have been poured into. If you are only buying one size, though, think big. A wineglass can never be too large.

Sparkling wines should be served in flutes, tall thin glasses with straight sides, so that the mousse or fizz is preserved. The old champagne saucers familiar from the films (and originally modelled, as the legend has it, on the breast of Marie Antoinette) are inefficient because the larger surface area causes higher dispersal of bubbles and flattens the wine more quickly. Having said that, I have to confess a sneaking fondness for them myself, at least for a more riotous occasion.

Fortified wines should be served in smaller, narrower versions of the ordinary wineglass in recognition of their higher alcoholic strength. The *copita,* traditional glass of the sherry region, is a particularly elegant receptacle and will do quite well for the other fortifieds too. Don't use your tiniest liqueur glasses, though; apart from looking spectacularly mean, they allow no room for enjoying the wine's aromas.

These three glasses (left) are all perfectly shaped for tasting. The one on the right is the official international tasting-glass.

DRINKING WINE *with* FOOD

Matching the right wine to its appropriate dish may seem like a gastronomic assault course but there are broad principles that can be easily learned. And very few mistakes are complete failures.

AT ONE TIME, the rules on choosing wines to accompany food seemed hearteningly simple. It was just a matter of remembering: white wine with fish and poultry, red wine with red meats and cheese, with sherry to start and port to finish. In recent years, that picture has become much more complicated, although its essential principles were mostly fairly sound. Today, magazines frequently run tastings to find wines that match a variety of increasingly exotic dishes, often created specifically for the article in question. One must not be surprised to find oneself, as I once did, trying to find a partner for a dish of sautéed duck livers sauced with strawberries and balsamic vinegar.

The exceptions to the original rules continue to multiply. Port is fashionable as an aperitif in France, the meatier types of fish, such as swordfish and tuna, are often found to go well with light reds, while it has now become almost a cliché to observe that most cheeses are happier with white wines than with reds.

Some abdicate all choice and happily drink champagne throughout a meal - fine for the goat's cheese salad and the turbot, not so great with the roast lamb.

The following are rough guidelines that incorporate some less obvious suggestions that you may not have thought of. At best, a particular partnership of wine and food adds up to something greater than the sum of its parts. At worst, a strongly flavoured food might strip the wine of some of its complexity, and make it taste rather ordinary - a phenomenon that becomes more distressing in direct proportion to the cost of the wine. But on the whole you can afford to be bold: very few combinations actually clash.

Pre-dinner nibbles with strong flavours such as Parma ham, olives and asparagus (below) are best served with a chilled fino or manzanilla sherry.

APERITIFS

The two classic (and best) appetite-whetters are sparkling wine and dry sherry. Choose a light, non-vintage champagne (blanc de blancs is a particularly good style to start things off with) or one of the lighter California or New Zealand sparklers. If you are serving highly seasoned canapés, olives or nuts before the meal, dry sherry is better. Always serve a freshly opened bottle of good fino or manzanilla. Kir has become quite trendy again: add a dash of cassis or other blackcurrant liqueur to a glass of crisp dry white (classically Bourgogne Aligoté) or to bone-dry fizz for a Kir Royale.

FIRST COURSES

Soups In general, liquidised soups are happier without wine, although thickly textured versions containing cream can be successful with richer styles of fizz, such as blanc de noirs champagne. A small glass of one of the nuttier-tasting fortified wines such as amontillado sherry or Sercial madeira is a good friend to a meaty consommé. Bulky soups such as minestrone may benefit from a medium-textured Italian red (Chianti or Montepulciano d'Abruzzo) to kick off a winter dinner.

Fish pâtés Light, dry whites without overt fruit are best: Chablis, Alsace Pinot Blanc, Muscadet *sur lie*, German Riesling Kabinett, young Viura from Navarra. But serve something more robust such as young white Rioja or fino sherry with the oilier fish like mackerel.

Chicken or pork liver pâtés Go for a big, pungently flavoured white - Alsace Gewurztraminer, California Fumé Blanc, Hunter Valley Semillon - or a midweight, soft red such as Valpolicella, Valdepeñas, a light *cru* Beaujolais like Brouilly or Chiroubles with a couple of years' bottle-age or red Sancerre.

Smoked salmon Needs a hefty white such as Gewurztraminer or Pinot Gris from Alsace, or an oak-fermented Chardonnay from the Côte de Beaune or California.

Melon The sweeter-fleshed aromatic varieties require a wine with its own assertive sweetness. Try noble-rotted Muscat or Riesling from Washington or California, or even young Canadian Ice Wine.

Prawns, shrimps, langoustines, etc Almost any crisp dry white will work - Sauvignon Blanc is a good grape to choose - but avoid heavily oaked wines. Go for high acidity if you are serving mayonnaise.

Deep-fried mushrooms Best with a medium-bodied simple red such as Côtes du Rhône or one of the lighter Zinfandels.

Asparagus Richer styles of Sauvignon, such as those from New Zealand, are perfect. Subtler wines will suffer.

Pasta dishes These really are best with Italian wines. Choose a concentrated white such as Vernaccia, Arneis or good Soave for cream sauces or those using seafood. Light- to medium-bodied reds from indigenous grape varieties work best with tomato-based sauces. Or you could try a Barbera or Sangiovese from California.

FISH AND SEAFOOD

Oysters Classic partners are champagne, Muscadet or Chablis. Most unoaked Sauvignon also makes a suitably bracing match.

Scallops Simply poached or sautéed, this most delicate of shellfish needs a soft, light white - Côte Chalonnaise burgundy, medium-dry German or New Zealand Riesling, Chardonnay from Alto Adige - becoming correspondingly richer, the creamier the sauce.

A crisply flavoured salad, such as this one with langoustines and avocado (above) needs an equally crisp, dry white wine to accompany it.

A delicate white fish dish such as paupiettes of sole (above) is best with a lightly oaked dry white wine.

The classic partner for coq au vin *(right) is a soft, mature burgundy - the region from which the dish originated.*

Lobster Cold in a salad, it needs a pungent white with some acidity, such as Pouilly-Fumé, dry Vouvray, Chablis, South African Chenin Blanc, Australian Riesling. Served hot as a main course (eg. Thermidor), it requires an opulent and heavier wine - Meursault, Chardonnay from California or South Australia, Alsace Pinot Gris, or perhaps one of the bigger Rhône whites like Hermitage.

Light-textured white fish Sole, trout, plaice and the like go well with any light, unoaked or very lightly oaked white from almost anywhere.

Firm-fleshed fish Fish like sea bass, brill, turbot or cod need full-bodied whites to match their texture. *Cru classé* white Bordeaux, white Rioja, Australian Semillon, California Fumé Blanc and most oaked Chardonnays will all fit the bill.

Monkfish Either a heavy, alcoholic white such as Hermitage or Condrieu or the biggest Australian Chardonnay, or - if cooked in red wine - something quite beefy such as Moulin-à-Vent, young St-Emilion, or even California Cabernet.

Salmon Goes well with elegant, midweight whites with some acidity such as *grand cru* Chablis, California, Oregon or New Zealand Chardonnay, dry Rieslings from Alsace or Germany. Equally, it is capable of taking a lightish red such as *cru* Beaujolais or Pinot Noir.

Tuna Go for a fairly assertive red in preference to white: well-built Pinot Noir (California or Côte de Beaune), mature Loire red (Chinon or Bourgueil), Washington State Merlot, Australian Shiraz, Chilean Cabernet, even Zinfandel.

MEAT AND POULTRY

Chicken If the bird is roasted, go for a soft-edged quality red such as mature burgundy, Crianza or Reserva Rioja or California Merlot. Lighter cooking treatments may mandate one of the richer whites, depending on any sauce.

Turkey The Christmas or Thanksgiving turkey deserves a show-stopping red with a little more power than you would serve with chicken. St-Emilion or Pomerol claret, Châteauneuf-du-Pape, Cabernet-Merlot or Cabernet-Shiraz blends from the USA or Australia will all oblige.

Rabbit As for roast chicken.

Pork Roast pork or grilled chops are happiest with fairly full reds with a touch of spice: southern Rhône blends, Australian Shiraz, California Syrah or the bigger Tuscan reds such as Vino Nobile or Brunello.

Lamb The meat that Cabernet Sauvignon might have been invented for, so go for the ripest and best you can find - from Bordeaux to Bulgaria, New Zealand to Napa.

Beef A full-flavoured cut such as rump or sirloin can cope with the biggest and burliest reds from anywhere: Hermitage, Côte-Rôtie, the sturdiest Zinfandels, Barolo and Barbaresco, Coonawarra Shiraz. Fillet steak needs something a touch lighter such as Bordeaux or a midweight Châteauneuf. Peppered steak or sauces containing mustard or horseradish call for an appropriate bite in the wine, either from Syrah or Grenache varietals or from the high acidity of Italian blends.

Duck A midweight red with youthful acidity to cut any fattiness is best: Crozes-Hermitage, Chianti Classico, California or New Zealand Pinot.

Game birds Best of all with fully mature Pinot Noir from the Côte d'Or, Carneros or Oregon, or - at a pinch - an aged Morgon.

Venison Highly concentrated reds with some bottle-age are essential. *Cru classé* Bordeaux or northern Rhône are the reference points. Cabernet, Shiraz and Zinfandel from hotter climates work well.

Offal Liver and kidneys are good with vigorous young reds such as Chinon, Ribera del Duero, Barbera or New Zealand Cabernet. Sweetbreads are better with a high-powered white such as a mature Alsace varietal.

DESSERTS

Fresh fruit salads are best served on their own, as there is generally too much acidity in them to do wine any favours. Similarly, frozen desserts like ice-creams and sorbets tend to numb the palate's sensitivity to wine. Anything based on eggs and cream, such as baked custards, mousses and *crème brûlée,* deserves a noble-rotted wine, such as Sauternes, Barsac, Monbazillac, Coteaux du Layon, the sweetest Vouvrays, or equivalent wines from outside Europe. Chocolate, often thought to present problems, doesn't do much damage to botrytised wines, but think maximum richness and high alcohol above all. Fruit tarts are best with a late-picked rather than rotted style of dessert wine, such as one of the lighter German or Austrian Rieslings, Alsace Vendange Tardive or late-harvest Muscat or Riesling from North America or the southern hemisphere. Meringues and creamy gâteaux are good with the sweeter styles of sparkling wine, while Asti or Moscato d'Asti make refreshing counter-balances to Christmas pudding. Sweet oloroso sherry, Bual or Malmsey madeira and Liqueur Muscat from Victoria are all superb with rich, dark fruitcake or anything nutty such as pecan pie.

Choose an assertively spicy red, such as a Syrah or Grenache, to accompany the peppery hotness of steak au poivre (left).

The chocolate sauce in poire belle-Hélène (below) doesn't have to present problems for wine if you go for a big, rich noble-rotted dessert wine.

LABELLING

ABOVE THE VINTAGE DATE on this German label, we see the rather complicated name of the estate proprietor, and below it the individual vineyard the wine comes from: Badstube in the village of Bernkastel. Below that is the grape variety, Riesling, and then the style, Kabinett - the least sweet of the QmP quality categories. Mosel-Saar-Ruwer is one of Germany's finest wine regions. To the left, the word *Erzeugerabfüllung* means "bottled by the grower". Note the typically low alcohol - 7.5%.

Wine labels from outside the European appellations have made a virtue of simplicity, so this South African wine simply tells us the name of the estate (Thelema), the vintage year (1994), the grape variety (Chardonnay) and the region of the country in which it was grown and produced (Stellenbosch). "Wine of Origin" is the rough equivalent of the French *appellation contrôlée*. Like many another hot-climate Chardonnay, the alcohol is high - 13.5%, reflecting the ripeness of the grapes.

Here is a wine intended to serve as an everyday brand from the portfolio of Lindemans. The label is as simple as can be. Australian winemakers often use bin numbers on their labels to refer to particular batches of wine, sourced perhaps from specific vineyards. Bin 65 is Lindemans' formula for an established blend of wines sourced from quite diverse regions, hence the geographically vague South Eastern Australia, which includes most of the country's grape-growing areas.

This California label has opted to put the regional and varietal identifiers higher than the name of the producer, since those will communicate most immediately to consumers (although there can't be many Californians who haven't heard of Robert Mondavi's wines). In the United States, a wine labelled with one variety like this has only to contain a minimum 75% of that grape, so there may in theory be other ingredients in it, but they must all have been grown in Napa.

The information on this Italian label is not substantially different from that on the German one. Reading down, we have the name of the individual vineyard (Vigna del Sorbo), then the producer (Fontodi) and then the appellation or denominazione (Chianti Classico, the heartland of Chianti). Then comes the quality level, or equivalent of AC - in this case Italy's highest, DOCG. Riserva here denotes a wine that has been aged for at least three years before release. Below that is the information that the wine has been bottled at the estate by its producer.

The practised eye begins to discern similarities between the labels of different European countries. On this Spanish label, we see the name of the producer (La Rioja Alta SA), then the brand name (Viña Ardanza), used to denote a particular blend in this case rather than an individual vineyard. *Embotellado en la propriedad* means "bottled on the estate". In the case of Rioja, Reserva denotes a wine that has been kept for three years before release, of which at least one must be spent in oak. The appellation is Rioja, below which appears the AC formula, DOC.

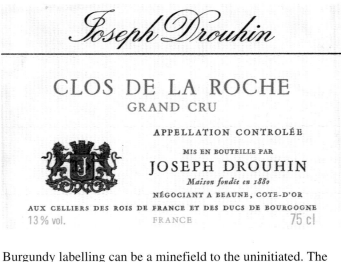

Champagne labels are rarely complicated. The house name will always dominate, since it is a form of brand, in this case Billecart-Salmon at Mareuil-sur-Ay. Above is the style, Brut being virtually the driest, and this one is pink. Champagne is the only AC wine that doesn't require the words *appellation contrôlée* to appear. Beneath the alcohol, the reference number of this house denotes that it is an NM (*négociant-manipulant*), a producer that buys in grapes and makes its own wine.

Burgundy labelling can be a minefield to the uninitiated. The merchant's name (Drouhin) is followed by the appellation. Clos de la Roche is one of the *grand cru* vineyards of the Côte de Nuits. This label at least tells you this is a *grand cru* wine, but doesn't have to state which village it belongs to (Morey-St-Denis, in fact). Note that *mis en bouteille* is not followed by *au domaine*, because it has not been bottled on an individual estate, but by a négociant or merchant based elsewhere.

GRAPE VARIETIES

Soil is furrowed the ancient way to catch winter rain (above), in the sweltering south of Spain.

S uch is the mystique and reverence attached to the appreciation of wine that it is easy to forget just what a simple product it is.

Visiting a modern winery today, with its acres of carefully trained vines, the giant tanks of shining stainless steel, the automated bottling line and perhaps the rows of oak barrels resting on top of one another in deep, cavernous cellars, you might think this was the end product of centuries of human ingenuity.

To the extent that the techniques for making good wine have been steadily refined through succeeding generations, indeed it is. Unlike beer, though, which had to await the discovery of malting grains before it could be produced, wine has always been there, for it is nothing other than spoiled grape juice.

Any substance that is high in natural sugars - whether it be the sticky sap of palm trees, or honey, or the juice of ripened fruit - will sooner or later start to ferment if it comes into contact with yeast. Wild yeasts, transported by insects and falling on to the fruit that they hover around, feed on its sugars and create two by-products in the process.

One is carbon dioxide gas, which is the reason why anything that has accidentally started fermenting creates a fizzy sensation on the tongue, and the other is alcohol. And we know what that does to us.

Long before the earliest human societies had begun to live settled existences in one place, and thus to cultivate land, a type of alcoholic liquid could be made relatively quickly by allowing fresh fruit to ferment.

One particular species of wild vine that originated in the area around the Black Sea that today takes in the modern states of Georgia, Armenia and eastern Turkey proved especially well-suited to quick fermentation, owing to the naturally sweet berries it produced. It is in fact the only vine species native to Europe and the Near East, and because it came to play such a pre-eminent role in the development of wine-making all over the world, it was later given the botanical classification *Vitis vinifera* - "the wine-bearing grape".

Within that one species, however, there are as many as 10,000 different sub-types, known as varieties. Some of these would have developed by natural mutation; many have been created by deliberate cross-fertilisation. Only a very small percentage of those 10,000 varieties are important in the commercial production of wine today, and many of those are fairly obscure. A mere handful, almost exclusively French in origin, now constitute the international language of wine, and it is these that this section deals with.

Not all of the 12 varieties we shall look at in detail are grown throughout the world, and the

A breathtaking springtime scene (right), with flower-ing mustard seed growing in the vineyards of Sonoma, California, the state that has become a major player on the world wine scene.

last of them - Gamay - is of no real viticultural significance outside its ancestral home, the Beaujolais region of France. But these are the 12 varieties - six white and six red - whose flavours it is most useful to become familiar with. They are responsible between them for producing all of the most famous French wine styles, from sparkling champagne in the north to the richly heady reds of the sweltering south, and thus they provided the original models when serious winemaking first began to be pioneered beyond the shores of Europe.

All sorts of other factors influence the taste of a wine than the grape variety or varieties from which it is made. The climate in which the grapes are grown determines the balance of sugar and acid in the harvested berries. In some still inadequately defined way, the type of soil the vines are planted in also has a crucial effect, in the opinions of many growers.

Then there are the many variables at work in the winery. At what temperature does the juice ferment? What does it ferment in - stainless steel or wood? How long, in the case of red wines, is the juice left in contact with the grape skins, from which it derives its colour and also the tannin that helps to preserve it? Is it kept in oak barrels after the fermentation? If so, are they new or used or a mixture of both, and how long does the wine spend in them before bottling?

There are as many styles of wine as there are winemakers, an equation multiplied by the number of different vintages each practitioner will make over the course of his or her career. But the identity of the grapes in the fermenting vat is the first and foremost indicator of style.

If you want to make a delicately crisp, simple white, it doesn't make sense to use Gewürztraminer. Similarly, if you're after a featherlight fruity red for drinking young, Cabernet Sauvignon may give you more than you bargained for. The most commonly met grape varieties have innate characteristics that can be teased out of the wines they are made into in wholly diverse parts of the globe.

As we are introduced to each of these 12 VIPs of the wine world, we shall also take a look at the different regions they have travelled to, and explore the typical flavours to be found in each of them.

The impressive vaulted cellars of Ch. de Meursault, in Burgundy's Côte de Beaune (above), filled with wine ageing in oak barrels.

CHARDONNAY

From its homeland in Burgundy, Chardonnay has travelled the world to become the most fashionable and sought-after of white varieties. This chameleon of grapes bows to the whim of the winemaker, offering a diversity of styles to appeal to all palates.

AS SOMEBODY once (nearly) said, if Chardonnay didn't exist, it would be necessary to invent it. No other grape, white or red, has achieved quite the degree of international recognition that Chardonnay has. In some consumers' minds, it stands as a synonym for dry white wine in general, and the reason is not hard to see. It is grown in some proportion in virtually every wine-producing country on the planet; within France itself, Bordeaux and the Rhône are about the only two regions that it has not yet penetrated.

No grape could have colonised the vine-growing world so effectively had it not possessed the adaptability of a chameleon. Given reasonably competent winemaking, it can usually produce something worth drinking, whether grown in the smouldering heat of South Australia or the precarious summers of the English Home Counties. In terms of the amount of land planted with it, Chardonnay is effectively the house white in the United States, Australia and New Zealand, not to mention the pays d'Oc in southern France.

The adaptability on which its huge commercial success is founded is twofold. In the first place, compared with most other grape varieties, it is something of a cinch to grow. Not only can it tolerate climatic conditions at either extreme of the viticultural spectrum, but it can make itself at home in a wide diversity of soil types without too much fuss. It is a fairly reliable ripener and gives a good crop in most harvests. Very fine wines, it is true, are almost invariably produced from vines that only give low yields, but as much of the Chardonnay that is sold around the world is intended for everyday drinking at economical prices rather than ageing in cellars, the vine's capacity to bear a lot of fruit makes it a winner.

Secondly, just as Chardonnay is everybody's flexible friend in the vineyard, so it proves similarly malleable in the winery. Unlike some of the other white grapes we shall encounter,

Chardonnay is not a naturally aromatic variety. Vinified very simply in stainless steel, and bottled early for drinking young, it doesn't possess a great deal of obvious personality. If it has any fruit aroma at all, it is generally a very faint appley quality, backed up perhaps by a refreshing streak of lemony acidity, but nothing more exotic than that. But it is precisely that neutrality that enables it to produce some of the world's most sought-after dry white wines.

Possibly more than any other white grape, it has a natural affinity with the flavour of oak. Matured in small new barrels, or even a mixture

Chardonnay matures in the warm vineyards of California (right). A vigorous vine, relatively unfussed by climate or soil, this golden grape is neutral in character and has a natural affinity with oak. It is as suited to classic white burgundies as to Australian sparkling wines.

of new ones and others that have been used for two or three vintages already, it begins to take on those richly creamy, buttery scents and tastes that we associate with really good Chardonnay. If the wine undergoes its initial fermentation in the barrels, in addition to being matured in them, it can derive a powerfully pungent smokiness from the charred inner surfaces of the wood that may remind you of anything from toast that's just beginning to burn to smoked bacon crackling in the frying-pan.

It is that ability to absorb the flavours of oak that originally made the top wines of Burgundy so esteemed, and accounts for the desire in other wine-making regions to imitate the full-blown oak opulence of Chardonnay *à la bourguignonne*. There is a feeling, however, in some quarters that the mania for oak flavours (which has resulted in small producers in less wealthy wine regions emptying bags of oak chips into

their wines to satisfy consumers' craving for that telltale taste of vanilla) is getting out of hand. The truth is that only the best-quality fruit from low-yielding vines represents a suitable case for the oak treatment. Grapes from younger, more vigorous vines will tend to produce less concentrated juice, so that oak fermentation leads to a wine that tastes of wood and nothing more.

As well as making the most popular styles of white table wine, Chardonnay is also indispensable to the production of sparkling wine the world over. With its two red partners, Pinot Noir and Pinot Meunier, it forms the triumvirate of grape varieties used in champagne, and nearly all attempts to produce classic sparklers outside that region use a healthy proportion of Chardonnay in their blends.

Once again, it is the grape's inherent neutrality of flavour that bestows elegance and finesse on the best fizz.

FRENCH ORIGINS
Almost all of the white wines of Burgundy, from Chablis down to Beaujolais. Champagne (where it makes up 100 per cent of wines labelled *blanc de blancs*). May appear as varietally labelled *vin de pays* across the south, especially Languedoc, and also in the Loire.

WHERE ELSE IS IT GROWN?
Wherever the vine will grow.

TASTING NOTES
Light and unoaked (eg. Chablis) - tart apple, lemon, sometimes pear. Lightly oaked (eg. Rully, St-Véran) - melting butter, baked apple, nutmeg, oatmeal. Heavily oaked (eg. Meursault, classic Australian Chardonnay) - vanilla, lemon curd, butterscotch, praline, bacon fat, woodsmoke.

Burgundy

If Chardonnay represents the monarch among white wine grapes, then the Burgundy region in eastern France is its official residence. From isolated Chablis in the *département* of the Yonne down to the wide swathes of vineyard known as the Mâconnais to the west of the river Saône, Chardonnay is the predominant white grape variety.

The entire gamut of styles is produced. There are easy-drinking everyday whites of honest simplicity as well as powerfully complex wines intended to be aged in the bottle. There are wines that rely on youthful acidity and freshness alone for their appeal, while others mobilise the fat, buttery opulence imparted by oak.

Co-operatives and négociants (merchants who buy in grapes or even finished wine from other growers and bottle the resulting blend under their own brand name) tend to be the sources for much of the commercial white burgundy seen in national drinks outlets, while the many individual producers who operate entirely self-sufficiently are responsible for some of the world's most extravagantly rich - and extravagantly expensive - dry white wine.

Chablis in some ways deserves to be considered as a region in itself, because it is not geographically part of Burgundy proper, lying as it does slightly nearer to the most southerly of the Champagne vineyards than to the northernmost tip of the Côte d'Or. Its climate is cool and fairly wet, its winters often severe, and late frosts in spring are a regular occurrence. As such, the Chardonnay grown there ripens quite late, and tends to produce a wine of high acidity, to which the adjective "steely" is often applied.

At their best, these are squeaky-clean, bone-dry wines that are crisp to the point of brittleness in their youth. Those used to warmer-climate Chardonnays may find them almost too acidic, but as they age, they lose some of that sharp edge and become mellower. That said, there is a general tendency to make softer wines these days.

The great majority of the wines are made without oak, Chablis being the reference for unwooded Chardonnay the world over. Some producers, however, do use a certain amount of oak on their best *cuvées*, particularly those with land in one or more of the seven *grand cru* vineyards - Blanchots, Bougros, Les Clos, Grenouilles, Preuses, Valmur and Vaudésir - that sit at the top of the quality tree. Even without oak, Chablis from a good producer in a fine vintage (such as 1988, '89, '90 or '92) can develop its own inherent richness with a few years in the bottle.

Southeast of Chablis, white wines from the Côte d'Or - and in particular the Côte de Beaune, its southern section - represent the pinnacle of Burgundian Chardonnay. It is here, in the exalted appellations of Corton-Charlemagne, Puligny-Montrachet, Meursault and others, that oaked Chardonnay really began.

The top wines, often produced in tiny quantities which helps to ensure they sell for dizzyingly elevated prices, are sumptuously rich and concentrated, usually deep golden in colour from months of ageing in oak barrels, and generally high in alcohol (13-13.5 per cent is the norm). Many possess an intriguingly vegetal flavour, like French beans or even cabbage, that is something of a shock to those used to

The rich, golden colours of a Burgundian autumn (below) spread through the sloping grand cru *vineyards of Vaudésir (nearest) and Grenouilles, in Chablis.*

fruitier-tasting Chardonnays. The Burgundians argue that this is their famous *goût de terroir* - the unique taste of the limestone soils in which the vines are grown.

It is still fair to say that wherever winemakers are aiming to produce premium-quality oaked Chardonnay, it is the top wines of the Côte d'Or that provided the original inspiration, however much they may since have diverged from that earliest model.

The Côte d'Or is connected to the Mâconnais by a strip of land called the Côte Chalonnaise, so called because it lies to the west of the town of Chalon-sur-Saône. Its Chardonnays, from appellations such as Montagny, Rully and Mercurey, are considerably lighter in style than those from further north, but can possess their own lean elegance. They tend to have correspondingly less oak than the Côte d'Or wines, and are thus suitable for more delicate white fish dishes.

In the south of Burgundy, the Mâconnais is the largest of its sub-regions. Here is where most of the everyday quaffing wine is made, much of it of rather humdrum quality, often vinified without oak. A couple of appellations stand out from the generality. Pouilly-Fuissé can have something of the depth and ageability of lesser Côte de Beaune wines, although quality across the board fails to justify the ambitious price it commands. St-Véran is cheaper but lacks that extra dimension of flavour that the best Pouilly-Fuissé has.

Certain villages within the overall appellation of Mâcon Blanc-Villages are considered to produce wines of sufficiently distinctive quality for their names to be added to the label; hence you may see Mâcon-Lugny, Mâcon-Viré and so forth on the labels. In most cases the quality difference from the catchall "Villages" designation is barely perceptible.

The white wine of Beaujolais, the most southerly of Burgundy's regions, is made from Chardonnay. Rarely seen outside its region of production, it tends to be hard, dry, and unoaked, somewhat like a less graceful version of Chablis.

Burgundy's sparkling wine - Crémant de Bourgogne, made by the champagne method - relies heavily on the Chardonnay grape. The grapes can theoretically come from anywhere in the region so styles vary from delicate, even slightly floral fizz to heavier wines that can have more than a tinge of that old green vegetable in the flavour.

Hand-picked Chardonnay grapes are loaded on to a trailer at Fuissé (above) in the Mâconnais, the largest sub-region of Burgundy.

United States

Wineries in New York State, especially those on Long Island (above), are increasingly producing elegant, complex Chardonnays.

Undoubtedly Chardonnay's most important home outside Europe is in the United States. Indeed, towards the end of the 1980s, the state of California alone had more extensive plantings of the grape than the whole of France, where its growth has not exactly been stagnant. No group of winemakers beyond the ancestral heartland of Burgundy has taken greater pains with the variety than the Californians, and the transformations that the wines have undergone in the last two decades have been a fascinating barometer of Chardonnay philosophy.

Twenty years ago, the fashion was for a massively overblown style of rich golden wine, with dollops of sweet new oak all over it, not dissimilar to the textbook Australian mode. When the backlash came, it sent the pendulum hurtling in the other direction, so that it suddenly seemed as if everybody was competing to produce West Coast Chablis, so lean and green and biting were many of the wines.

By the mid-1980s, the picture was beginning to even out, and there is now a much greater diversity of styles, each representing a more relaxed expression of its microclimate and the orientation of the individual winemaker.

The very best Stateside Chardonnays - such as those from the cooler areas of California like Carneros and Sonoma Valley, from Oregon, even from New York State - can sometimes achieve an almost eerie similarity to certain top burgundies, partly because of the comparable levels of acidity, and partly because of the sensitive use of French oak.

A lot of work has been done in researching types of oak, and the different levels of flame treatment the cooper can give the barrels, to find out what best suits American Chardonnay. Some producers, veterans of trips to Burgundy, put their faith in the supposedly more sophisticated flavours of French oak, but others are now beginning to look once again at native American woods and are starting to disprove the theory that you can't make a subtle Chardonnay in US oak.

Another French habit that has taken root among many of the premium producers is the avoidance of the filtration procedure whereby tiny solids that are residues of fermentation are cleaned out of the wine. While filtering a wine certainly results in a crystal-clear, stable product, many feel that it also strips it of some

Madonna Vineyards in the cool Carneros region of northern California (right), a region that produces some of the state's finest Chardonnays, eerily similar in style to certain top burgundies.

of its flavours and some of its richness of texture. As the debate has grown in intensity, the anti-filtration brigade has often proudly inscribed the word "Unfiltered" on its labels.

Despite the studious awareness in the States of how things have traditionally been done in Burgundy, there is increasingly less dependence on that region as a role model. American winemakers have carved out a niche in the world market for their Chardonnays to the extent that they no longer need the reflected glory of comparison with the Côte d'Or.

It is no more possible to generalise about a typical California style than it is to talk about a French style. The state contains a multitude of different microclimates: Calistoga, at the northern end of Napa Valley, is one of the hotter areas, as is the inland San Joaquin district; Santa Barbara, one of the more southerly grape-growing regions, is relatively cool.

Most of California's coastal regions are affected by the Pacific fog drifts that can take until mid-morning or later to clear. Cool night-time conditions help to ensure that the ripening grapes don't become heat-stressed, so that acidity levels at harvest time are not too low.

Good California Chardonnays have the same sort of weight in the mouth as a wine like Puligny-Montrachet, and with a carefully

defined balance of oak and fruit. Acidity is usually fresh, though with perhaps not quite the same tang as young burgundy. The fruit flavours are altogether more overt, California wines often having a riper citrus character, even a tropical element like fresh pineapple. By and large, despite what some producers intend, they are not particularly susceptible to improvement in the bottle. Most will never be better than they are at one to two years old.

In the Pacific Northwest, Oregon Chardonnay tends to be crisper and slightly more austere on the palate than the wines of California, and the characteristic style is leaner and less ostentatious. Washington State is improving all the time, with the earlier tendency to slight flabbiness now being erased in favour of some attractively balanced wines, though again with somewhat less flesh than California examples. Idaho has a more extreme climate, and tends to produce wines with high acidity, though they can be rounded out by gentle oak treatment.

New York State has a much cooler climate than the West Coast, and the Chardonnays it produces are in a correspondingly more bracing style, but the best wineries - notably on Long Island - are capitalising on that to turn out some elegant and complex wines with some ageability.

Chardonnay is also gaining in importance in Texas, where it makes a broad, immediately approachable style with plenty of ripe fruit.

Chardonnay ageing in new oak barrels (above). A lot of research has been carried out in the US to find out which oak best suits American Chardonnay, leading to a trend among certain producers away from French oak to native American oak.

Australia

Such was the soaring popularity of Australia's Chardonnays on external markets in the 1980s that, at one stage, it began to look as if the country might not be able to produce enough to cope with the worldwide demand for them. One consequence is that there is now more Chardonnay planted across the continent than any other white grape variety.

With the advent in this decade of the "flying winemakers" - travelling wine consultants who flit between the hemispheres working as many vintages as they can fit into their schedules - the success of Australian wine had received the global endorsement that it was due.

Many of the flying winemakers came from Down Under and, though it often involved a great swallowing of cultural pride on the part of the natives, they were instrumental in revolutionising winemaking practices in the viticultural backwaters of southern France. It was their skill with Chardonnay that, more than anything, served to create the demand for their services.

Australia taught the wine world that Chardonnay could be as unashamedly big and ripe and rich as you wanted it to be. Since the climate in most of the vineyard regions, the majority of which lie in the southeast of the country, is uniformly hot and dry, the fruit grown there regularly attains sky-high levels of natural sugar. Winemakers thus generally have to sharpen their wines up by controlled additions of tartaric acid to prevent them from tasting too sweet.

Nonetheless, the benchmark style of Chardonnay is a sunshine-yellow, extraordinarily luscious wine that, married with the vanilla and butterscotch flavours of new oak, is quite a way off being fully dry. High sugar means high alcohol (up to 14 per cent in some wines) so that, at the end of a generous glassful, you certainly know you've had a drink.

As British wine consumers (and many American ones too) discovered an almost insatiable thirst for Australian Chardonnay, it became the habit in some quarters to start calling into question whether these wines really possessed true balance.

In Australia, there is a long-established system of regional wine shows, where wines are judged with scrupulous attention to detail by experts from the industry, and lessons and inspiration are drawn from the results. It has been suggested that, under the conditions of having to taste many similar wines over a number of days, tasters will inevitably be most easily won over by those wines that make the boldest impact on the palate - ie. those with the heaviest oak influence, the most alcohol, and therefore the ones that linger longest on the palate after tasting.

The response to this can only be a personal one. Undoubtedly, classic Australian Chardonnay is a commercially popular style, and it is always hard to argue with that. But it should be remembered that framing the debate in those terms also gives a conveniently simplistic view of the matter.

In latter years, trends in Chardonnay have begun to diversify in Australia just as they have in California. There is a desire on the part of many winemakers, notably in Western Australia, in South Australia's Coonawarra region and in the Yarra Valley in Victoria, to make a subtler, more European - or perhaps more Californian - style of Chardonnay.

Carpets of purple flowers surround Mountadam Estate (below) on the High Eden Ridge, in South Australia. Eden Valley, part of the Barossa Range, shares the soils and climate of Barossa Valley, the source of richly concentrated Chardonnays.

While that move to greater refinement may represent the future, I suspect it will be a long while before wine-drinkers grow tired of the blockbuster Chardonnays that put Australia on the wine map. They constitute, after all, one of the world's truly unique white wine styles.

Much of Australia's wine is made from grapes grown in different areas, blended to get the best balance of attributes in the final wine, so regional characteristics can only be significant to the extent of their proportion in the bottle. However, an increasing number do bottle wines that are the produce of particular vineyard areas, vinified separately so as to give a true expression of what the French would call their *terroir*.

In the state of South Australia, the Barossa Valley is one of the most important regions, producing broad-beamed, richly concentrated Chardonnays that make a dramatic impact on the palate. McLaren Vale and Padthaway are responsible for wines with perhaps a touch more finesse. The Clare Valley is distinctly cooler, and its wines are correspondingly lighter and less upfront in style.

Chardonnays from the Goulburn Valley area of Victoria often possess hauntingly tropical fruit characters, while the cooler-climate Yarra Valley wines can resemble those of the cooler parts of California. In Western Australia, the Margaret River region is producing some unashamedly Burgundian wines that sometimes have that pungent whiff of green vegetable found on the Côte d'Or.

On the island of Tasmania, Chardonnay can be more austerely European still in its orientation, owing to the cool and fairly wet climate. Levels of grape acidity comparable to Chablis are not unheard of.

Stormy skies at first light (above) over the high ridges of the Barossa Range, South Australia.

New Zealand

(Above) Montana Estate, Marlborough, South Island. New Zealand Chardonnay is light, with juicily ripe fruit.

Like its northern neighbour, New Zealand now has more Chardonnay planted than any other white wine grape. Grown in what is a considerably cooler and damper climate than Australia, the wines it produces tend, on the whole, to be noticeably lighter and more acidic.

That doesn't mean to say that Chardonnay lacks anything in terms of character because, in common with the even more fashionable New Zealand Sauvignon Blanc, it nearly always possesses a positively unearthly degree of juicily ripe fruit. It is quite the norm to find pineapple and mango, grapefruit and apple chasing each other around the glass, almost as if the wine had

set out to confound the notion that Chardonnay isn't an aromatic variety.

About the richest styles come from the Gisborne and Poverty Bay regions on the eastern tip of the North Island, and these are the ones that respond best to oak-ageing. A little to the south, the wines of Hawkes Bay have more of a tang to them, and require a correspondingly more delicate touch with the wood.

Hopping over to the South Island, edging in the direction of the Antarctic Circle, the typical style becomes snappier and more citric in Marlborough, and then quite taut and austere from Canterbury and Otago.

South Africa

The lush green vineyards of Stellenbosch wineries Warwick Estate (above), and Thelema Vineyards (right), producers of rounded, golden Chardonnays. Coastal Stellenbosch is home to many of South Africa's finest producers.

When South Africa began to play a full part on the international wine scene at the beginning of the 1990s, many consumers were surprised to discover that Chardonnay was not the major force that it is elsewhere in the southern hemisphere. It played second fiddle to the much more widely planted Chenin Blanc. It still accounts for only a very small percentage of the vineyard land planted with white varieties, although that will presumably increase as it has done just about everywhere else.

Although South Africa remained largely isolated from world trade while the wine boom of the 1970s and 1980s was gathering momentum, it did profit in one respect. It was able to observe

the trend for the galumphing, heavily oaked style of Chardonnay (at first inextricably associated with so-called New World winemaking) as it fell from favour among forward-looking winemakers, and simply pass that fad by.

How the wines will taste depends inevitably on how far the vineyards lie from the southern coast. Those from further inland have the hotter climates. Thus, the Robertson Valley - over 100km (63 miles) away from the cooling maritime influence of the Indian Ocean - is home to some of the Cape's biggest and brassiest Chardonnays, while those from Walker Bay achieve a subtler style with the emphasis on fruit and more sharply defined acidity.

Rest of the World

SOUTH AMERICA

Chile's Chardonnays, as with its Cabernet Sauvignon wines, occupy two pigeonholes. Some are made in a recognisably French vein, with pronounced acidity, light appley fruit and carefully judged oak maturation. Others go the whole hog, with full-blown charred oak flavours and a high-extract, alcoholic feel. It all depends on the producer. Argentina's wines, made largely in the province of Mendoza in the foothills of the Andes, occupy a midway point between those two extremes.

EUROPE

Increasing concentrations of Chardonnay are cropping up across northern Italy now, from Piedmont in the northwest to the Veneto in the northeast. Although some rugged individualists are aiming for top-flight barrel-fermented wines (and charging energetically for them), the basic style - best typified by the wines of Alto Adige on the Austrian border - are delicate, very lightly creamy wines made without the use of wood.

Northern Spain is getting in on the act too, with plantings of Chardonnay vines in Penedés, Lerida and Navarra, where it is often blended with local varieties to make clean-cut, nutty, dry modern whites.

Chardonnay is of increasing importance in central Europe, particularly in Hungary where the flying winemakers have been regular visitors. The wines tend to be made in the straightforward neutral style, clean and sharp for everyday drinking. When they do have some oak on them, it is only to add a gentler, rounder feel to them.

Further east, Bulgaria has been making Chardonnays for export since its heavily state-subsidised entry into western markets in the 1980s. A little on the clumsy side, they often don't taste especially fresh, although the odd wine from the Khan Krum region in the east of the country can be palatable in a sour-cream sort of way.

Chardonnay is taking root in northern Italy, especially in Piedmont (above), in the foothills of the Alps, where it produces delicate, lightly creamy wines.

Harvesting Chardonnay grapes (left) in Blatetz, Bulgaria. The quality of Chardonnay, one of many wines produced for the export market, varies, some of the best coming from Khan Krum.

CABERNET SAUVIGNON

Its pedigree is firmly founded in the gravelly soils of the Médoc, in the heart of Bordeaux. The king of red grapes, Cabernet Sauvignon has conquered vineyards across the world without losing the classic character that brought it such renown.

THE RED HALF of that hugely successful partnership that has come to dominate international winemaking is the Cabernet Sauvignon grape. Alongside Chardonnay, it strode imperiously through the world's vineyards in the 1980s, often insisting that native varieties get out of its way wherever serious red wine was to be made. Although the example held up to Cabernet growers - the classed-growth clarets of the Médoc in Bordeaux - is an illustrious one, it isn't immediately easy to see why Cabernet came to be perceived as the pre-eminent red counterpart to the crowd-pleasing Chardonnay.

Its adaptability to different soils and climates is certainly quite as impressive as that of Chardonnay, yet the number of berries the vine typically yields, even in the warmest climates, is relatively low. Since that obviously means it can provide less wine than many of those native varieties that ceded precious vineyard land to it, it bore a heavy responsibility to earn its keep.

In many regions, particularly those subject to marked climatic variation from one year to the next, Cabernet Sauvignon was basically a loss-leader. For the sake of having its name on the label, many winemakers simply tightened their financial belts and allowed their higher-volume wines to subsidise it.

What the sacrifices were about was achieving that heady mixture of pure blackcurrant fruit, density of texture and substantial ageing capacity that the best Cabernet Sauvignon wines combine, and that seems to many consumers the essence of all that is noble in a red wine. The greatest productions of the Médoc - Lafite, Latour, Margaux, Mouton-Rothschild - are among the most famous names in wine, and if some of the class of those wines could be seen, however distantly, in a Cabernet Sauvignon from Chile, Italy or Bulgaria, then the winemaker behind it might have a fair chance of making the big time.

Like Chardonnay too, Cabernet responds supremely well to oak ageing, when the vanillin in new wood helpfully serves to soothe some of the natural ferocity of the young wine. That ferocity is basically tannin, the substance in youthful red wine that furs up the drinker's mouth and can obscure the natural flavours of the fruit. It is derived from the pips and skins of the grapes, and Cabernet Sauvignon is particularly well-endowed with regard to those parts of its anatomy. The small berries the vine puts forth mean that the pips constitute a higher proportion of the grape than in other varieties, and it is famously - notoriously, some have found - thick-skinned.

Indispensable for producing handsome, deeply-coloured red wine, those thick skins do however mean that vinifiers of Cabernet need to make some finely detailed decisions in the winery about how to treat their wine. Allow the crushed skins to soak for too long in the juice, and you can end up with fearsomely tannic, merciless morning-after stuff, and there isn't much point in advising customers to keep it for a decade if that is not what your market positioning is about.

What many producers of Cabernet wine have gradually learned, and the lesson was there in the original Bordeaux model, is that Cabernet Sauvignon is much better off in company; that is, blended with at least a small proportion of one or two other grapes. Left to its own devices, it too often comes out tough and brutal, whereas a carefully judged admixture of (classically) Merlot and/or Cabernet Franc, or (innovatively) Shiraz in Australia, can soften and civilise it without in the least lessening its austere beauty.

The holy grail is a wine capable of acquiring distinction from long cellaring. Cabernets or Cabernet-based wines react in fascinatingly various ways as they age, depending on the quality of the fruit prior to fermentation, on the type of wood used for the maturation and on the length of time the wine spends in barrel (and perhaps subsequently in bottle in the winery) before being released. As the initial tannins start to loosen up and dissolve into the wine, the first

The small, dusty-blue Cabernet Sauvignon grape (right), produces wines of good tannin, body and aroma. It adapts easily to differing soils and climates, and in its finest form, with warm, late summer sun to ripen it fully, Cabernet creates complex, deeply coloured reds, packed with juicy blackcurrant fruit.

FRENCH ORIGINS

Bordeaux, specifically the left bank of the river Gironde, from the north of the Médoc down to the Graves. (On the right bank, it tends to play second fiddle to Merlot.)

WHERE ELSE IS IT GROWN?

Just about everywhere, although it has not made significant inroads into the cooler climates of northern Europe.

TASTING NOTES

In warm climates, almost any of the purple-skinned fruits - classically blackcurrants (perhaps most startlingly so in the best wines of Chile), but also black plums, brambles, damsons, etc. Often has a distinct note of fresh mint or even eucalyptus, especially in parts of Australia and Chile. Cooler climates can create a whiff of bitterness in it, often uncannily like chopped green pepper. Oak treatments generally emphasise a mineral austerity in the wine, likened in Bordeaux to the smell of cigar-boxes, cedarwood or - most recognisably - pencil shavings. With several years' bottle-age, it can take on aromas such as well-hung game, plum tomatoes, warm leather, dark chocolate, even soft Indian spices like cardamom, while the primary fruit begins to taste more like preserved fruit.

fresh flavours of the grape - known to tasters as primary fruit - begin to take on other aromas and tastes that may be reminiscent of dried fruits, savoury spice or gamey meat. Even at quite advanced stages of development, though, the telltale mineral purity of Cabernet Sauvignon still shines through.

It is this potential for gathering complexity that explains the high prices paid for top Cabernet Sauvignon around the world, and that also explains the enormous pains taken with the variety by all sorts of winemakers who might be able to turn a faster buck growing something more mundane.

Bordeaux

A landmark in the Pauillac vineyards of first growth Château Latour (above), one of the five great premier cru *châteaux of the Médoc.*

The chai *at Château Mouton-Rothschild, Pauillac (below). The four famous communes of the Médoc - St-Estèphe, St-Julien, Margaux and Pauillac - are where the reputation of red Bordeaux is founded.*

Although Cabernet Sauvignon occupies far less vineyard land in its home base of Bordeaux than its traditional blending partner Merlot, it is nonetheless widely considered the pre-eminent variety in the region. This is because it plays a major part in the wines on which the reputation of Bordeaux is founded - the *crus classés*, or classed growths, of the Médoc and Graves. When the classification system for Bordeaux was drawn up in 1855, it was not that the judges ignored the Merlot-based wines of Pomerol and St-Emilion on the right bank; they simply didn't consider them to be in the same class.

That classification (which we shall look at in further detail in the chapter on Bordeaux) is now considered seriously outdated by many commentators, but the general perception that the majority of Bordeaux's most illustrious wines derive the greater part of their authority from the presence of Cabernet Sauvignon has never really changed.

Cabernet contributes those austere tannins that give the young wine the structure it needs to have a good chance of ageing. Its pigment-rich skins endow the wine with full-blooded depth of colour. When claret-lovers refer to their favourite wine as having a profoundly serious quality that appeals first and foremost to the intellect rather than the senses, it is Cabernet Sauvignon they have to thank.

If Cabernet enjoys such an exalted status, you may ask why more châteaux don't simply produce an unblended Cabernet wine instead of making it share the bottle with Merlot and other varieties. The answer is partly that the grape works better in a team. Solo Cabernet, as some winemakers in California have found, is not necessarily an unalloyed blessing. In hot years, it can just be too much of a good thing, the resulting wines having colossal density and concentration, but not really seeming as if they are going to be ready to drink until the next appearance of Halley's comet.

The other reason for blending in Bordeaux is that, even though its southerly position makes this one of the warmest of France's classic regions, the summers are still highly variable. In problem vintages (and it is worth bearing in mind that, despite its phenomenal run of luck in the 1980s, Bordeaux did not have an overall success in any of the years 1991, '92, '93 or '94) Cabernet Sauvignon is the grape that suffers most. If the end of summer is cool - and, what's worse, wet - it simply doesn't ripen properly, resulting in those vegetal green-pepper tastes that make for harsh, depressing wine.

Since Merlot has much better tolerance for less-than-perfect vintage conditions, it makes sense for the growers to have the option of blending in some of the lighter Merlot to soften

an overly astringent or green-tasting Cabernet. In the great vintages, however - such as 1989 and '90 - the richness and power of Cabernet is worth celebrating, and the Merlot will only play a discreet supporting role, just smoothing the edges a little so that the full glory of ripe Cabernet can be shown to maximum advantage.

Most of the wines that occupy the five ranks of the 1855 hierarchy come from four vineyard areas to the west of the river Gironde: St-Estèphe, Pauillac, St-Julien and Margaux. From top to bottom, collectively, they extend over not much more than 40km (25 miles), but there are subtle differences in the styles of Cabernet-based wine they produce.

St-Estèphe generally makes the fiercest wine, with typically tough tannins that may take years to fall away, and a very austere aroma that is often compared to fresh tobacco. Pauillac - the commune that boasts three of the five first growths in Lafite, Latour and Mouton-Rothschild - is a little less severe, even when young. Its wines have more emphatic blackcurrant fruit than those of St-Estèphe, and a seemingly more complicated pot-pourri of spice and wood notes as they age.

St-Julien, which adjoins Pauillac, displays many of the characteristics of its neighbour, although its wines somehow display a softer fruit - more like dark plums and blackberries than blackcurrants - as they begin to mature. The best wines of Margaux are noted for their extravagant perfume, although in general the

underlying wine is lighter than anything from further north, the exception being first-growth Château Margaux itself.

South of the city of Bordeaux, the large area of the Graves makes wines that vary in character. These range from featherweight reds that constitute some of the region's lightest reds, to those that have a mineral earthiness to them, thought to derive from the gravelly soils that give this part of Bordeaux its name. Elsewhere, the quality becomes gradually more prosaic until, at the lowest level of AC Bordeaux, the wines can be hard red jug-wine of no great appeal.

In Bordeaux, it is the name of the property rather than the name of the producer that goes on the label. Much time and attention is devoted to studying the relative form and fitness of the most famous estates as each new vintage appears on the market. Those planning to buy even a single bottle of top-flight Bordeaux would do well to consider the present reputation of a château as well as the quality of the vintage.

Cabernet Sauvignon vines (above) planted in the poor, gravelly soils of St-Estèphe, in the Médoc, on the right bank of the Gironde river.

United States

Cabernet Sauvignon was introduced to California in the 19th century in the form of cuttings from Bordeaux. The readiness with which it took to the fertile soils in which it was planted is evidenced by the fact that it already had something of a reputation among the American wine cognoscenti before the century was out. The best was held to come from the Napa Valley, north of San Francisco, where the late, hot summers resulted in strapping great wines of swarthy hue, thickly textured and capable of delivering a hefty alcoholic blow to the unsuspecting drinker.

Some might facetiously say that not much has changed. Certainly, in many consumers' minds, the benchmark style of California Cabernet has been fiercely tannic, often virtually black wines that potentially took a decade or two to unravel into anything like a state of drinkability. It would be grossly simplistic to characterise all California Cabernets in that way today, but it was undeniably the predominant style of the wine as recently as the 1970s, and there are undoubtedly some wineries that still nail their colours to that particular mast.

It is not as if, however, there are not perfectly good antecedents for it. Most classed-growth Bordeaux in the hot years like 1989 and 1990 would answer that description - or something very like it - when first released. The wines are not intended to be drunk straight away, however much the French predilection for youthful red wine seems perilously close to infanticide to other wine-drinking cultures. California's winemakers were aiming high after all, and Cabernet Sauvignon doesn't come much higher than Château Latour, still black as sin and guarded by snarling tannins at ten years old.

The problem lay in the fact that most consumers did not wish to drink wine that tastes like that, even if they could readily afford the exorbitant price the achievement of such concentration demands. Producers realised a middle way had to be found between the extremes of budding West Coast Latours and insipid commercial jug wine.

Thus the 1970s saw a huge upsurge in plantings of Bordeaux's most celebrated variety in all sorts of diverse microclimates across the state, as Cabernet fever took hold.

The winery at top Napa Valley producer, Robert Mondavi (below). Napa Valley, in Sonoma County, is renowned for the world-class Cabernets it can produce.

Picking Cabernet Sauvignon grapes in vineyards south of Prosser, Washington State (left). Despite the fairly cool climate, some fine Cabernets have been made in the Pacific Northwest.

Statue at sunset (above) in the gardens of the Robert Mondavi Winery, Napa Valley, California.

Some of the resulting wines, notably those from the cooler areas, have more than a touch of the familiar bell-pepper/asparagus/French bean vegetal quality that the grape is prone to when its juice has not had sufficient ripening time. Maturation times in oak barrels have sometimes been excessive, giving wines an exaggeratedly woody taste.

But without a doubt, California - and especially the Napa Valley - has also turned out some wonderfully sleek, opulently fruit-filled Cabernets of world-class status, many of them blended with others of the Bordeaux varieties.

In the Pacific Northwest, the climate is generally a little too cool for producing great Cabernets, although Washington State has come up with some fine examples. The tendency is to compensate for less than generous fruit flavours by applying fairly heavy oak maturation, which can run the risk of creating top-heavy wines. Oregon is a much safer bet for cool-ripening Pinot Noir than sun-seeking Cabernet.

Texas, on the other hand, is proving itself to be highly Cabernet-friendly, although as yet the grape only accounts for a relatively small proportion of total plantings there. The state style - exemplified by wineries like Fall Creek and Pheasant Ridge - is of big, rich, upfront fruit, some savoury herb character and good weight, but with the tannins kept in check. In time, this could emerge as the best American Cabernet territory outside the Napa Valley.

Australia

Australia's approach to Cabernet Sauvignon has arguably been much more straightforward than that of California. The aim among its growers is all about emphasising the kind of ripe, juicy drinkability that wins friends even among those who don't consider themselves fans of rich red wine. In the ultra-reliable climates enjoyed by most of Australia's wine-growing regions, Cabernet more often than not attains levels of ripeness Bordeaux's producers would give their eye teeth for.

Oak barrel ageing is used enthusiastically by the great majority of Cabernet growers. When your wine is as rich and dense and blackcurr-anty as most Australian Cabernet is, you can afford to be generous with the oak flavours. At the same time, however, the familiar style aims to maximise fruit characters without extracting too much tannin from the grapeskins. Thus, although an intensely concentrated wine, it doesn't necessarily scour your mouth with harsh astringency when it's young.

The chances are that, even if you are unfamil-iar with the winery, a Cabernet from practically anywhere in Australia will deliver plump, soft, cassis-flavoured wine with an engaging creamy texture and no hard edges. That is not to say

that there aren't wineries intent on producing wines in a more austere style that are built to age, but even these will come round far sooner than most California Cabernets or Cabernet-based clarets made in the same idiom. A classic example is South Australian winery Wynns' top Cabernet, John Riddoch, a ferociously dark wine of massive concentration. Even tasted in its infancy, the tannins on it are nowhere near as severe as the colour may lead you to expect.

The John Riddoch that Wynns' best Cabernet is named for was the wine-grower who, in the last decade of the 19th century, first planted grapes in a part of South Australia called Coon-awarra. Coonawarra's chief distinguishing feature is a narrow strip of red soil the colour of paprika known as *terra rossa*. It is here that Cabernet Sauvignon produces its most gor-geously distinctive performances in Australia.

The wines often have a chocolatey richness to them, tinged with hints of coffee bean like mocha. Some, noting the relatively cooler cli-mate the region enjoys, have compared the region to a southern-hemisphere Bordeaux, but Coonawarra stands in no need of such vicarious honour. Its wines are nothing like claret; they have their own uniquely spicy style.

Endless rows of Cabernet Sauvignon vines under an endless Australian sky (below), in Clare Valley, South Australia. The hotter, drier climate encourages rich, dense Cabernets.

South Australia is the most important state for Cabernet Sauvignon wines. In the heat of the Barossa Valley, they tend to be richly coloured and thickly textured, with an intensity like bottled fruits. From McLaren Vale, the wines are often more delicately proportioned, with slightly higher acid levels. In the Eden Valley, Cabernets of almost European profile are being produced, with aromatic spice notes in them, and often a dash of mint.

Coonawarra, discussed above, takes that spice component a little further, and there is a lean elegance to the wines that full-fleshed Cabernets from hotter regions can lack. Riverland is a much less distinguished bulk-producing region where the wines are made in an easy-drinking, uncomplicated style.

Victoria makes Cabernet in the leaner, mintier style. The vineyards are mainly located in the centre of the state, especially in the increasingly fashionable district of Bendigo. Despite its notably cool climate, Yarra Valley has been responsible for some of Australia's most talked-about Cabernets.

Cabernets from the Margaret River area of Western Australia also tend to the subtly scented end of the spectrum, rather than the blockbuster fruit-essence idea. Acidity is particularly good and the wines are consequently quite long-lived.

Tasmania's cool, damp climate is better suited to other varieties, but the large-scale Heemskerk winery has scored some successes with lighter, more sharply angled Cabernets than are found on the mainland.

The famous terra rossa *soil of Coonawarra, South Australia (above). Vineyard land here is highly prized for the quality of grapes it yields.*

Other Non-European

NEW ZEALAND

Most of New Zealand's vineyard land has proved to be too cool and damp for Cabernet Sauvignon, which is notoriously bad-tempered if it doesn't get enough sun. Some varietal Cabernet has achieved a refreshing fruitiness, more loganberries or even raspberries than the textbook blackcurrant, but the telltale green-pepper flavours of cool-climate Cabernet have marred too many wines. Acidity tends to be high, but at least tannin is usually low. They are generally wines for short-term drinking, rather than the long haul.

New Zealand's most conspicuous successes have been with Bordeaux blends, where real complexity and depth in a midweight style not a million miles from the softer wines of Bordeaux can be very attractive. Te Mata Coleraine and the Cabernet-Merlot blend from Cloudy Bay are the two obvious show-stoppers.

The towering Drakensteinberg mountains form a stunning backdrop to the higher and cooler district of Franschhoek in coastal Stellenbosch, South Africa (below), source of classy Cabernets capable of ageing.

SOUTH AFRICA

Cabernet Sauvignon became, in the early 1990s, the most widely planted red grape variety in South Africa. Although many winemakers are lavishing all the care and attention on the grape to which it is accustomed elsewhere, the results have so far not been an unqualified success. Many of the wines have been marred by a muddy, not particularly fruity character. This is partly due to the specific variant of the Cabernet mostly grown on the Cape, and partly to the grapes suffering heat stress in some of the world's hottest vineyards.

In the right hands, though, there are some convincingly classy wines that have proved capable of ageing. Nederburg, Stellenryck and the Reserve wines of Avontuur stand out from the crowd. The best regions so far have been coastal Stellenbosch and inland Paarl. As with New Zealand, wines made from the Bordeaux blend, using Cabernet Franc and Merlot to soften some of Cabernet Sauvignon's severity, tend to be the best: Warwick Farm Trilogy and Meerlust Rubicon are just a couple of noteworthy examples.

CHILE

During the course of the 1980s, Chile was a kind of southern-hemisphere epicentre for European wine consultants, and no variety was more consulted on than Cabernet Sauvignon. When no less an eminence than Gilbert Rokvam of Château Lafite arrived at the Los Vascos winery, it seemed pretty clear that Chile had made its entrance on the world wine map with a vengeance, at least as far as Cabernet was concerned.

What has happened since is that Chilean Cabernet has diverged into two broadly identifiable styles. One is what Europeans love to think of as the benchmark New World style, ripely blackcurranty Cabernet of sumptuous, velvety texture with low tannins and plenty of oak. The Montes winery's top Cabernet, Montes Alpha, and some of the Reserve bottlings of Caliterra are typical examples.

The other style is much more austere, cedary wine of high acidity and more pronounced tannins, vinified in a way that is intended to help it to age in the bottle, and owing much to the taste of classic Médoc claret. Prime movers here are Los Vascos, Cono Sur and the celebrated Antiguas Reservas wines of Cousiño Macul.

At its best, Cabernet Sauvignon wine from Chile can possess some of the most intensely pure essence of blackcurrant found in any red wine produced anywhere. Too often, though, that fruit quality is obscured by over-extraction of tannin, or it is simply rendered dilute by allowing the vines to bear too many grapes, resulting in unfocused flavours. Despite such aberrations, Chile is slowly but surely on the way to becoming a world-class producer of some pedigree Cabernets.

ARGENTINA

On the other side of the Andes, the Mendoza province of Argentina is beginning to show its own potential as a major runner in the Cabernet stakes. Strangely enough, it is a red grape called Malbec - one of the bit-part players in red Bordeaux - that is the star of the show, with Cabernet still very much its understudy.

Initially, varietal Cabernets were rather sternly tannic, and dominated by wood flavours as opposed to fruit on account of their having been aged for too long in old oak casks. Far less outside investment poured into Argentina compared with what was happening in Chile in the 1980s, and so the wines, Cabernet Sauvignon in particular, have taken time to find the right style to make the rest of the world take note.

Led by the quality-conscious Trapiche, Norton and Weinert operations, Cabernet is now being made in a generally French-oriented style, with the rich plum and cassis fruit backed by savoury herb flavours and a judicious amount of tannin. Cabernets from the recently established Cateña Estate could turn out to be the best of all.

Harvesting Cabernet Sauvignon at Los Vascos (above) in the hot Colchagua Valley, Rapel, Chile. Los Vascos produces Cabernets moulded in the classic Médoc style.

Old Cabernet Sauvignon vines owned by the grand 19th-century bodega, Cousiño Macul (left), in Maipo, Chile. The vines date back to the 1930s.

Other European

Pickers on the Marqués de Griñon's estate near Toledo, in the hot centre of Spain (above). The estate has drawn attention for its structured, long-ageing Cabernets.

The Torres Mas la Plana vineyard in Penedés, planted solely with Cabernet vines (below). Torres and Jean León set a precedent for Cabernet in Spain in the '60s.

FRANCE

Just outside Bordeaux, in appellations such as Bergerac and Buzet, the permitted grape varieties are the same as in Bordeaux itself, and from certain producers (notably the large co-operative at Buzet) the wines can rival middle-of-the-range claret. Cabernet Sauvignon has now made inroads into the experimental zone of Languedoc-Roussillon, on France's warm south coast, where it appears as varietal Vin de Pays d'Oc, with very patchy results to date.

SPAIN AND PORTUGAL

Cabernet Sauvignon established a bridgehead on the Iberian peninsula when it was planted in Penedés by the Torres family and Jean León in the 1960s. Although the León wines have tended to the mellow and approachable axis, both the Black Label wine of Torres and - even more so - the Marqués de Griñon Cabernet, from near Toledo, are made in the opaquely concentrated, towering style for long keeping.

Many producers, in regions such as Ribera del Duero and Costers del Segre, are experimenting with blending amounts of Cabernet Sauvignon in with Spain's indigenous superstar grape, Tempranillo - often with exciting results.

The same philosophy towards blended wines has tended to be followed by those Portuguese growers who have planted Cabernet, although there are some accomplished varietal wines produced on the Setúbal Peninsula south of Lisbon, notably from José Maria da Fonseca. Quinta da Bacalhoa is a noted Bordeaux blend made in an unmistakably Portuguese idiom.

ITALY

Italy's growers have traditionally tended to be a little cavalier, particularly in the northern regions, in distinguishing Cabernet Sauvignon from its Bordeaux sibling Cabernet Franc. Thus, a Trentino wine labelled "Cabernet" may be one or the other, or both. Yet these two grapes are quite different and produce distinct styles of wine.

Less confusion arises in Tuscany, where Cabernet Sauvignon is allowed to make up a minor part of the blend in Chianti, and in lesser-known reds such as Carmignano. A revolution in Italian wine was effected in the 1970s by a group of Tuscan innovators, led by the highly respected family house of Antinori. They began working outside the Italian wine regulations to produce monumental reds that made free use of Cabernet Sauvignon, either blended with the Chianti grape Sangiovese - such as Piero Antinori's Solaia - or with the other Bordeaux varieties, as in the case of his brother Lodovico's Ornellaia.

Cabernet has also gained a foothold in Piedmont in the northwest, with trailblazer Angelo Gaja producing an ostentatious unblended Cabernet called Darmagi.

CENTRAL AND EASTERN EUROPE

The cheap red wine boom in the 1970s and 1980s was sustained almost single-handedly by the state-subsidised exports of Bulgaria. For a supposedly marginal wine-making culture, Bulgarian Cabernets generally offered the sort of easily lovable, softly plummy fruit flavours that producers of cheap Bordeaux can only dream about. The wines were smoothed with plenty of oak and were often released as "Reserve" bottlings after several years' ageing in the state cellars.

At their best, these wines managed to combine enough depth of character to grace a serious dinner table, with the sort of instant drinkability that made surefire party wines. Sadly, the break-up of the old state monopoly immediately resulted in wild inconsistencies in quality but, with a little investment, Bulgaria may well come back into contention.

Hungary, Moldova and Romania are all capable of producing good Cabernet at a price the wine-drinker wants to pay. Hungary's Villany and Romania's Dealul Mare look the most promising regions so far.

Other Cabernet-based one-offs include the legendary Chateau Musar of Lebanon, a blend of Cabernet with Cinsaut made in the Bekaa Valley by the indefatigable Serge Hochar. Where other winemakers worry about problems like spring frosts, Hochar has had to contend with the siege conditions imposed on swathes of the Middle East by war, invasion and rocket attacks. That the fruit of his labours is a magnificently long-lived and powerful wine is a due tribute to his determination.

Chateau Carras, from the foothills of Mount Meliton in Thrace, is Greece's convincing attempt at a claret-style blend, aided and abetted by Bordeaux wine professor Emile Peynaud.

Bulgaria's vineyards, like these overlooking the village of Ustina, near Plovdiv (above), were the source of much commercially successful Cabernet in the 1980s.

SAUVIGNON BLANC

The grape of the famous Loire whites, Sancerre and Pouilly-Fumé, Sauvignon also brought New Zealand to the attention of the wine world, with a fruit cocktail of a wine, that proved the versatility of this variety.

IF CHARDONNAY is the first white wine grape that consumers get to know, then Sauvignon Blanc tends to be the second. In many ways, that is because its characteristics can be seen as diametrically opposed to those of Chardonnay. Whereas Chardonnay is typically seen as a golden-hued, fat-textured, oaky white wine with whatever aromatic personality it possesses being derived from the influence of wood, Sauvignon is a pale, relatively light and acidic wine most often vinified without oak and endowed with a piercingly distinct perfume.

A well-made Sauvignon performs its role as light refreshment almost too well. The simplicity of this style has led some to treat the variety with mild contempt. This undoubtedly does the grape a great injustice - it is in fact capable of impressive complexity. Sauvignon is responsible for two of France's most celebrated dry white wines - Sancerre and Pouilly-Fumé; when the vine's yields are controlled, it displays a wealth of uninhibited ripe fruit flavours, one of the most pleasing attributes a white wine can boast, as shown by the great success of New Zealand Sauvignon.

In addition to its upfront fruit, Sauvignon grown on certain flinty soils in the upper Loire valley in the centre of France can take on an inexplicable but oddly powerful smoky quality that deceives many into thinking it must have had some oak treatment. At its most pungent, it can resemble the savoury fume of woodsmoke; in a gentler vein, it may remind you of the wisps of steam from an espresso machine. This attribute is celebrated in the second half of the name of Pouilly-Fumé (although it only makes its presence felt in a minority of the wines), and it came to be much imitated in the California of the 1970s when Napa Valley winemaker Robert Mondavi renamed his Sauvignon wine Fumé Blanc.

Wines labelled Fumé Blanc made outside France generally tend to rely on some oak fermentation and/or maturation to achieve the

The green Sauvignon Blanc grape (right), here in Pessac-Léognan where it is destined for blending with Sémillon for the dry white Bordeaux. A prolific vine, but when yields are controlled it is capable of massive fruit character.

elusive smokiness. If a hot climate and excessively high yields have reduced some of the natural varietal intensity of Sauvignon, then the influence of charred oak can seem a handy, if expensive, way of putting it back. Whether Sauvignon responds well to ageing in oak has become one of those debates that periodically convulses the wine world. The California trend for making an almost sweet-seeming, though

technically dry, style of oaked Sauvignon has since been imitated in Bordeaux, where the grape almost certainly originated, so the issue can't be presented as a straightforward scrap between Europe and America.

Just as Cabernet Sauvignon finds its compatible bedfellow in Merlot, so the Sauvignon Blanc often gets on famously with Sémillon - a grape that, as we shall see in due course, is rapidly assuming an individual reputation of its own. Nearly all white Bordeaux, whether dry or sweet, contains some Sauvignon, and the proportions are likely to increase since the region has seen a tremendous upsurge in plantings of the variety as it has become internationally trendy.

More than any other region outside France, it is New Zealand that has done wonders for the worldwide status of Sauvignon. It may very well be that, across the board, New Zealand's winemakers now have a better understanding of the grape than the French. Nor do their Sauvignons necessarily sell at dissuasively high prices on the export markets as many of the French versions do. Mouthful for mouthful, New Zealand Sauvignons offer more ecstatically happy fruit flavours than practically any other dry white wines in the world.

In general, Sauvignon Blanc is lost without a decent level of good crisp acidity, which is why, in very hot areas, it results in a rather flabby and fruitless wine. Many Australian Sauvignons have suffered from precisely this problem.

FRENCH ORIGINS
Bordeaux, where it is nearly always blended with Sémillon (and perhaps a drop of Muscadelle). The upper Loire valley is where France's top varietal Sauvignons are based, and less exalted wines are made further west along the Loire in Touraine.

WHERE ELSE IS IT GROWN?
Fairly widespread, but particularly important in New Zealand, and somewhat less so in the United States, Australia and South Africa. Isolated plantings in the warmer Languedoc and northern Spain are beginning to prove surprisingly successful.

TASTING NOTES
Practically the whole gamut of fruit flavours, ranging from sour green fruits like gooseberry and tart apple or pear to astonishingly exotic notes such as Charentais melon, passion fruit and mango. It very often has a precise nose of blackcurrants. Vegetable flavours can loom large too. Green peas, asparagus and sweet red peppers often crop up in New Zealand examples. Then there is a curiously pungent animal quality in many cool-climate, especially Loire, versions that is often compared to cat's pee, or even to male sweat. If you're lucky, that fugitive wisp of faintly acrid smoke is there as well.

France

LOIRE

In the vineyards around the upper reaches of the river Loire, in the centre of France, unblended Sauvignon Blanc reigns supreme. It wasn't that long ago that these crisp, scented dry white wines, designed to be drunk within a couple of years of harvest, were not especially highly regarded even within France itself. As fashion shifted momentarily away from the richer and oakier styles of white in the 1960s, Loire Sauvignon - Sancerre in particular - found itself catapulted to the height of popularity.

Pouilly-Fumé and Sancerre are the two most famous appellations for Sauvignon. They are situated on opposite sides of the river, on the east and west banks respectively. It is a very accomplished taster indeed who can spot one from the other, both capturing, as they do at their best, the combination of refreshing green fruit flavours, snappy acids and distant smoky aromas that typify the grape in these parts.

The fashionability of the wines elevated their prices in the 1970s, and they have never really come down again. For wines of such great cachet, it has to be said that there are too many indifferent producers, notably in Pouilly-Fumé. Gitton, Mellot and Bourgeois are reliable names in Sancerre, Dagueneau and de Ladoucette in Pouilly-Fumé.

To the west of Sancerre are three minor appellations for the Sauvignon grape. They offer something of the flavours of their more exalted neighbours while possibly just lacking that final dimension of concentration. The best, and closest to Sancerre, is Ménétou-Salon (where Henry Pellé is the outstanding grower). Further west, across the river Cher, Quincy and Reuilly produce brisk, assertive Sauvignon in a clean but less elegant style than the others.

In the heartland of the Loire region, the Touraine district - more famous for its Chenin Blanc wines - also has a lot of Sauvignon. A fair amount of it gets used as blending fodder, but some varietal wines are bottled under the label Sauvignon de Touraine. In good years, they too can offer a glass of cheerfully fruity white, without anything like the intensity of the wines of the upper Loire.

Early-morning mist (above) over Sauvignon vines in the Loire's famous Pouilly-Fumé appellation.

The village of Sancerre (right) that gives the appellation its name stands on a hilltop close to the river Loire, overlooking the vineyards.

BORDEAUX

The dry white wines of Bordeaux were dragged kicking and screaming into the modern world during the 1980s. Too often stale and dispiriting creations based on over-produced Sémillon, they have benefited hugely from the trend towards colder fermentations using temperature-control equipment.

As Sauvignon wines from further north gained in modishness and therefore retail value, it dawned on the Bordelais that perhaps they could cash in on the Sauvignon mania by vinifying more of what was after all one of their own main grapes. The percentage of Sauvignon in many of the blends has accordingly noticeably increased, bringing in its train a greater freshness and zip to the wines.

Top of the quality tree is the region of Pessac-Léognan at the northern end of the Graves, where a healthy scattering of wines from properties such as Domaine de Chevalier and Châteaux Haut-Brion and Laville-Haut-Brion show true class. Some producers use only Sauvignon in their whites: Couhins-Lurton, Malartic-Lagravière and Smith-Haut-Lafitte can be magnificent. The smart operators have used barrel-ageing (and even fermentation in oak as well) in order to achieve a rich, tropical-fruit style that is far more opulent than the unoaked Sauvignons of the Loire.

The large production of the Entre-Deux-Mers region is generally more humdrum stuff, although the occasional wine can shine. Château Thieuley, in the west of the region, makes an oaked and unblended Sauvignon to rival the best of Pessac-Léognan. Sauvignon also plays a supporting role in the great sweet wines of Bordeaux, to lend a flash of balancing acid to the noble-rotted Sémillon.

ELSEWHERE

The Bergerac appellation, on the river Dordogne, has the same grape varieties as Bordeaux and can turn out some light, refreshing Sauvignon-based blends, as can the Côtes de Duras to the south. White wines labelled Vin de Pays des Côtes de Gascogne, from further down in southwest France, may be made from any of a number of grapes, and there is a smattering of varietal Sauvignon among them.

Although it may seem inauspiciously hot, the increasing plantings of Sauvignon in the Languedoc are yielding some attractively crisp, fruity Vins de Pays d'Oc that owe their super-fresh quality to cold fermentation in stainless steel. Chais Baumière and La Serre have made two of the better wines seen in recent years.

Finally, there is a lone outpost of Sauvignon in the far north of what is technically the Burgundy region, near Chablis. Sauvignon de St-Bris is an historical oddity, best described as tasting like Sauvignon made in a Chardonnay style, with the recognisable green fruit but smoother contours than are found in the Loire versions. Because the traditional white grape around here is Chardonnay, the wine is only accorded VDQS status, one rung down the ladder from *appellation contrôlée*.

In the Sauternes region, as here at Château Suduirat (below), Sauvignon Blanc brings a streak of fresh acidity to balance the sweetness of noble-rotted Sémillon.

New Zealand

The Cloudy Bay winery in New Zealand's Marlborough district (below), one of the country's greatest success stories with the Sauvignon grape.

Sauvignon devotees weaned on the exhilarating flavours of New Zealand's finest efforts may be surprised to learn that it is only the third most widely planted grape in the country. It is easily outnumbered by Chardonnay and the common-or-garden German variety Müller-Thurgau. New Zealand Sauvignon shot to prominence in the 1980s on the back of the wine made by the bulk-producing Montana winery in Marlborough on the South Island. The commercial success of its Sauvignon Blanc - always a harvest festival of pure raw-fruit ripeness - was founded on its sheer exuberance of flavour, and shored up over the years by the fact that its export price has hardly moved. This despite the fact that few wines have further to travel to the international marketplace than those of southern New Zealand.

Having sparked a trend, Montana's example was quickly followed by a host of other wineries. That surge of abundant fruit is present in nearly all of the wines of the Marlborough region, although occasionally the acidity can be out of focus, or - as in the troubled vintages of 1992 and '93 - just a little too aggressive. Some of the most sensationally concentrated fruit of all has been seen on the wines of Jackson Estate, Wairau River and the Oyster Bay range from Delegat's, while Hunters Estate and the famed Cloudy Bay (which is blended, Bordeaux-style, with a dash of Sémillon) achieve a textural depth as well that renders the wines unbelievably lush.

That slightly softer style of Sauvignon really comes into its own in the North Island region of Hawkes Bay. The fruit seems less green and more peachy, and there is a correspondingly greater readiness to use oak in the vinification, though by no means universally. Vidal's Sauvignon is one of the more opulent Hawkes Bay examples, with Castle Hill from the Te Mata winery also showing well. Villa Maria, although not based in the region, makes a fine, competitively priced Sauvignon from fruit grown there.

Other Regions

AUSTRALIA

The hotter the wine region, the less likely it is to be capable of producing the appetising fruit and natural crispness that Sauvignon wines need. Australia has consequently made some of the least sharply defined Sauvignons around. One of the best - Cullens - comes, not unexpectedly, from the cooler Margaret River region of Western Australia, while Mount Hurtle, in McLaren Vale, makes an appealingly fruity version.

UNITED STATES

Robert Mondavi's attempt to elevate the status of California Sauvignon by renaming it Fumé Blanc has still not managed to persuade other growers to take the variety to their hearts. Dry Creek Vineyards in Sonoma makes an impressively ostentatious one, as does Ferrari-Carrano. Sterling Vineyards is gradually moving towards a steelier Loire-like style of Sauvignon, albeit using a small percentage of barrel fermentation in the wine. Many other growers, if they have Sauvignon at all, try to disguise what they see as an embarrassing herbaceousness in the flavour of the grape by ageing in oak or else leaving a distracting quantity of residual sugar in the wine.

CHILE

There is a large, and for the time being intractable, problem with Sauvignon Blanc in Chile, which is that a lot of it isn't. Quite a few growers planted a grape called Sauvignon Vert or Sauvignonasse thinking it was the Loire variety, whereas it is in fact the dullish, neutral-tasting relative of a grape native to northeast Italy. Despite the confusion, these wines are still likely to be labelled Sauvignon Blanc, so there is no way to tell what you're likely to get. One of the best, and most definitely the real thing, is Casablanca Santa Isabel, from one of Chile's cooler growing regions. The Carmen winery's Reserve Sauvignon is also good.

SOUTH AFRICA

As elsewhere, it is the cooler areas that do best with Sauvignon, the Constantia and Durbanville regions around Cape Town being the most promising. Some co-operative wines from further north in the hotter Swartland district can be surprisingly crisp, if not exactly a riot of fruit.

The Cullens winery in the Margaret River area of Western Australia (above) has consistently produced one of the country's more sharply defined Sauvignons.

Chile's cooler Casablanca Valley (left) is proving a good spot to grow characterful Sauvignon Blanc.

PINOT NOIR

Difficult to grow, difficult to vinify but still producers across the globe are attracted to this temperamental grape variety, tempted to try matching the classic style of Burgundy's greatest red wines.

OF ALL THE French grape varieties that have migrated around the viticultural world, this is the one that excites the greatest passions. More tears are shed, greater energy expended, more hand-wringing despair engendered over it than over any other variety.

Almost every serious grower outside those areas where plantings of the grape aren't permitted (and even some within) would like to produce a fine Pinot Noir at some stage in their careers, and such is the challenge involved in it that many would settle for only ever producing one. It is not, by and large, an endeavour for those who relish a quiet life.

In the beginning, it was all so simple. Pinot Noir is the only grape permitted in the great majority of red burgundy (the only exceptions being at the bottom of the quality ladder). At the summit of Pinot ambition sit the *grand cru* wines of Vosne-Romanée on Burgundy's Côte d'Or, wines of positively exotic complexity that offer a once-in-a-lifetime experience of sumptuous richness at a once-in-a-lifetime price. All the red-wine appellations of the Côte d'Or, however, are capable of producing great Pinot at one time or another - they don't call it the Golden Hillside for nothing.

So there is the model for the world to emulate. Why all the heartbreak?

Initially, the almost insuperable obstacle seemed to be that Pinot Noir just couldn't be coaxed into producing the same sorts of flavours that it is able to achieve in Burgundy. It most emphatically doesn't take to hot climates. Grown in the kinds of conditions that Cabernet Sauvignon loves, it results in horribly muddy wines, often with the flavour of sub-standard fruit being boiled up for jam.

Burgundy itself is cool and wet, prone to spring frosts and even hailstorms. The lesson seemed simple enough. Plant it in similar environments elsewhere and maybe it could be persuaded to yield up its charms.

The first attempts in the cooler areas of the United States, Australia and New Zealand, however, didn't seem to suit it either. Now it came over all green and bitter, full of off-putting vegetal pungency and a streak of hard, spiteful acid that made it a powerful repellent to consumers. Pinots produced in these conditions were among the feeblest red wines in the fine wine sector, and the labour of love that had been lavished on them with so little reward meant that they had to be sold for stupidly high prices.

What was being discovered was that Pinot is much more choosy about where it will grow than those other cosmopolitan vines, Chardonnay and Cabernet. Not only does it want the right weather, but it has a distinct partiality for soils with some limestone in them. Even at its

Ripe, healthy bunches of Pinot Noir grapes (right). A thin-skinned grape that is highly sensitive to climate and soil, and notoriously difficult to nurture, Pinot Noir can make ripely fruity reds of great class. It is also invaluable in the production of sparkling wine.

ripest, it is a thin-skinned variety - physically as well as temperamentally - which means that it is more prone to vine diseases than most, and rots very easily if the vintage has to take place in persistent rain.

The potential pay-off, if conditions are exactly right, is that, because of those thin skins, Pinot produces a generally lighter wine than Cabernet. Because there is less tannin to be extracted, the wines tend to be approachable earlier in their development (although it pays to wait for the naturally high acidity to settle down a bit) and they mature faster. Good Pinot can be a memorable experience at six or seven years old - although the best will continue to improve for substantially longer - whereas the finest Cabernets are still clenched shut and full of sulking tannins.

Increasingly, producers outside Burgundy have got the hang of it in recent years. In California and the Pacific Northwest of the US, the dedication and viticultural intelligence of a hard core of growers has demonstrated more conclusively than anywhere else that Pinot can thrive

outside its native Burgundy. After all, once the overall conditions are established, it should be possible to produce more good Pinot more often than in climatically chaotic Burgundy, where the conservative estimate is that two vintages in every three are not really suitable for the production of decent wine.

As a result, the emphasis of the Pinot debate has now shifted to what the optimum style of the wine should be. Put simply, there are two schools of thought: one school opts for deeply coloured, ripely scented wines full of red fruit but possessed of fairly big beefy texture, while the other wants to achieve the lighter, earthier-smelling brews liable to turn gamey with age. This latter wine is associated with the old-fashioned style of the Côte d'Or. Don't think of this as a straight fight between Americans and Burgundians, though. There are examples of both styles in each camp.

Additionally, Pinot Noir plays an important role in the production of champagne and other sparkling wines, where it adds depth and longevity to the Chardonnay and colour to the rosés.

FRENCH ORIGINS
Burgundy and Champagne. Also used in some of the light reds and rosés of the Loire, and the red wine of Alsace.

WHERE ELSE IS IT GROWN?
California, Oregon, Australia, New Zealand, a little in South Africa. Quite important in central Europe - southern Germany, Switzerland, and points east - but still fairly rare along the Mediterranean. Anybody making sparkling wine by the traditional champagne method is likely to use some Pinot.

TASTING NOTES
In youth, it can possess light aromas of red fruits, typically raspberry, strawberry, maraschino cherry. In parts of California and Australia, it also has a faint note of coffee bean or mocha. Nearly always has an element of meatiness - beef stock in young wines, shading to well-hung game as it ages, overlaid in the very best with the other-worldly pungency of black truffle. Classically (or notoriously, depending on your tastes) mature wines can also display a distinctly rank smell, politely described as "barnyardy", but really referring to what you might accidentally put your foot in as you walk through the barnyard.

France

Levelling Pinot Noir grapes in the traditional wooden press at Champagne Bollinger (above).

Harvested Pinot Noir grapes resting in traditional wicker baskets (below) at Louis Latour, in Aloxe-Corton on the Côte d'Or, the home of most of Burgundy's famous names.

Betting on vintage conditions in Burgundy as harvest-time approaches makes for slightly more peace of mind than playing Russian Roulette - but not much more. In most years, the region's white grape variety, Chardonnay, fares reasonably well: only torrential rain during the picking can really ruin it at the eleventh hour. Pinot Noir, the only runner in the red wine stakes, is a different kettle of fish.

It is no exaggeration to say that, more often than not, Pinot Noir yields disappointing results. Precisely because out-and-out successes are so hard-won, great red burgundy has come to be valued by many as the most precious wine of classical France, consort to Bordeaux's monarch, but held in special esteem because of its rarity.

The Pinot grape reaches the apex of its potential on the Côte d'Or, the narrow escarpment running southwest of the city of Dijon, and home to most of Burgundy's famous names. The narrower northern strip, the Côte de Nuits, which includes such appellations as Gevrey-Chambertin, Nuits-St-Georges and Morey-St-Denis, tends to produce the weightiest style of Burgundian Pinot, with all sorts of meaty notes ranging from the singed skin of roasted fowl to gravy bubbling in the dish. Further south, the Côte de Beaune, which takes in Aloxe-Corton, Pommard and Volnay among others, specialises in a lighter, gentler Pinot, smelling of soft summer fruits and sometimes flowers as well.

The further south of the Côte d'Or you travel, into the Côte Chalonnaise and then the work-horse region of the Mâconnais, the more ordinary the Pinot Noir wines become. At the bottom of the scale, wine labelled Bourgogne Rouge may be a blend of grapes from different sources in the region and covers a multitude of sins, as well as the occasional happy surprise.

If the vintage has been particularly chilly, or worse doused with rainfall as in 1991, the resulting wines can be extremely light, both in colour as well as in texture. When a red wine is full of hard acids and bitterly unripe fruit, and feels no richer on the palate than a heavyish rosé, then consumers have a tough time seeing why they should pay the inflated prices.

On the other hand, if burgundy is noted for one thing, it is a resistance to generalisations. Some producers - Joseph Roty in Gevrey-Chambertin, to take one random example - managed to make densely concentrated wine in 1991, while others were wringing their hands. It pays to know who the high fliers are.

Because Pinot often lacks adequate natural sugar to ferment into a full-bodied red that will stay the distance, producers are permitted to add ordinary cane sugar to the freshly pressed juice. The process is known as chaptalisation, after its inventor Jean-Antoine Chaptal. By giving the yeasts more sugar to work on, the potential alcohol content of the finished product is raised. The average strength of red burgundy is a stiffish 13 per cent. Sometimes, especially when young, it can give off a telltale whiff of burnt sugar, a probable indicator that the winemaker has resorted to fairly heavy chaptalisation.

In the best vintages, however, such as the happy trio of 1988, '89 and '90 - known in France as *les trois glorieuses* - when the Pinot Noir has attained full ripeness, the wines it is turned into are richly perfumed, exquisitely elegant creations that go some way at least to justifying the heart-stopping prices they sell for.

Although it is a red grape, Pinot Noir is hugely important in the making of champagne. The colourless juice is vinified without its skins so that the resulting wine remains white, although if you compare a blended champagne with one that has been made entirely from the region's only white grape, Chardonnay, you will notice a deeper, nuttier hue in the one that contains Pinot

Autumnal Pinot Noir vines (left) running down towards to the town of Aÿ, in Champagne. The inclusion of Pinot in champagne lends it a nuttier, darker hue, and gives the wine depth and good ageing potential.

The beginnings of a red burgundy - Pinot Noir gently fermenting in an open wooden vat (above).

Noir. Champagne producers consider that Pinot gives their wines depth and the ability to age well. Some champagne, labelled "blanc de noirs", is made entirely from Pinot Noir and the region's other red grape Pinot Meunier, but is still a white wine. A small amount of still red wine, vaguely Burgundian though even more crisply acidic in style, is made, and may be added to white wine to make rosé champagne. Tiny quantities of pink champagne (such as Laurent-Perrier rosé) are made by the painstaking method of infusing the red grape skins briefly in the white juice to tint it to the desired shade.

In the eastern Loire, Pinot Noir is used to make the red and rosé versions of Sancerre and Ménétou-Salon. These are much lighter in style than top burgundy, often with a slightly vegetal hint like cabbage leaves. They are not intended for ageing but, served slightly chilled, can make good summer drinking.

Pinot Noir also makes the only red wine of Alsace, again in a typically featherlight not overly fruity style, although attractive, perfumed examples from the likes of Zind-Humbrecht and particularly Marcel Deiss provide the exceptions that prove the rule.

United States

CALIFORNIA

This has undoubtedly been the most successful region across the board for Pinot Noir outside Burgundy itself. Although they are extremely unlikely to admit it, Burgundy's producers could profitably learn a fair bit from the approach of the most conscientious growers of Pinot Noir in America.

The most successful area to date has been Carneros, a cool district straddling Napa and Sonoma Counties and benefiting from the coastal fogs that waft in from San Francisco Bay. The afternoons and early evenings in Carneros are sufficiently warm to endow the developing grapes with the exciting flavours of ripe red fruits that are characteristic of the best Pinot wines. At the same time, the cooling influence of those thick mists that often hang around until mid-morning ensures adequate levels of fresh acidity, so the wines are impeccably balanced and capable of ageing.

Its ripe fruit intensity means that California Pinot Noir is generally ready for drinking earlier than traditional burgundy, although it does benefit from keeping for a year or two after release just to allow the nervy edge on those acids to calm down. If it had a noticeable problem during the 1980s, the period when the wine

Terracing a new Pinot Noir vineyard in Oregon (below). The grape of Burgundy is making itself at home in the Pacific Northwest.

world was beginning to abandon its presumption that Pinot Noir was not a suitable occupation for a non-European winemaker, it was that the levels of alcohol were a touch high. That often resulted in wines that were very attractive until you swallowed them, whereupon they left a slight smouldering at the back of the throat. Today, the balance is a lot better.

In addition to Carneros, where producers like Saintsbury and the low-profile Kent Rasmussen have scored some considerable triumphs in recent vintages, parts of Santa Barbara County south of the Bay have proved promising for Pinot Noir. Au Bon Climat and Sanford are both wineries to watch here. The mountainous inland region of San Benito is home to the pace-setting Calera Winery, whose Pinot is regularly among the most stunning from California.

OREGON

Because of its cooler, damper climate, this Pacific Northwestern state was seen as ideal Pinot territory when the search for appropriate vineyard sites began to gather momentum. Climatically, it is undoubtedly much closer to Burgundy than most of California, and yet the results have not so far been an unqualified success. It remains to some extent a tale of unfulfilled potential.

In some cases, yields from the vines have been allowed to go too high, a vice that Pinot Noir is very unwilling to forgive. Mainly, though, the problem has been that the fruit just hasn't quite attained the state of ripeness conducive for good wine. If you emulate Burgundy's environment too closely, after all, you may end up duplicating the same handicaps that spoil too many of its wines.

That said, Oregon enjoyed a succession of great vintages in the late '80s and early '90s, and some wineries are now beginning to show just what thrilling Pinots Oregon is capable of making. The Reserve wines of Bethel Heights have been sublime, while Domaine Drouhin - an Oregonian outpost of one of the great Burgundy merchants, where the wine is actually made by a member of the Drouhin family - broke into the super-league with its 1991 Pinot Noir. The style is generally lighter than in most of California, less meaty but with more accentuated strawberry fruit.

Other Regions

NEW ZEALAND

The coolest wine climate in the southern hemisphere should be nicely hospitable for Pinot Noir. Although there are not many superstars as yet, New Zealand should soon be well on the way to producing some top-flight wines from this grape. Best so far have been Martinborough Vineyards, Palliser Estate and Ata Rangi, all displaying the savoury intensity that adds complexity to the familiar red fruits.

AUSTRALIA

As with other cool-climate grapes, it is crucial to find the right site for Pinot Noir in Australia, in order to avoid the muddy or jammy characters that can so easily spoil it. The Yarra Valley in Victoria fits the bill because of its altitude (Yarra Yering and Coldstream Hills have both made richly satisfying Pinots in this area). In the centre of Victoria, the Bendigo district is home to a winery called Passing Clouds, which has made some fine, thickly-textured Côte de Beaune-style wine. Moss Wood, in Western Australia's cool Margaret River region, is making great strides, while on Tasmania, Piper's Brook produces some of the most Burgundian Pinot Noir outside France.

SOUTH AFRICA

As in Australia, much of the country is simply too hot to achieve great elegance in wines made from Pinot Noir, and the grape is not that important in South Africa. The coastal Walker Bay region, however, boasts two world-class producers in Hamilton-Russell and Bouchard-Finlayson (the latter a joint venture with one of the major Burgundy companies).

GERMANY

In Germany, they call it Spätburgunder, and it has long been a traditional grape for the very small amount of red wine the country is able to produce. The typical style is light as a feather and not much further on from rosé. Although the northerly region of Ahr somehow contrived to get itself a reputation for red wines, Baden in the south seems considerably more auspicious for wines of decent fruit. Some of the young, innovative producers are beginning to coax some concentration and depth out of German Pinot Noir, but the quantities involved have so far been very modest.

A layer of plastic sheeting is used to insulate Pinot Noir grapes growing in the Hollenburg vineyard in Germany's Rheingau region (above).

Hand-plunging the grape skin cap on a tank of Pinot Noir (left) at the Yarra Yering winery in Victoria.

SEMILLON

To many producers, Sémillon suffers a lack of individuality that has destined it to be blended with more fashionable varieties. Yet as the source of rich, golden, honeyed Sauternes, and the unique, aged dry white of Australia, Sémillon is second to none.

WHILE IT IS undoubtedly one of the world's foremost grape varieties, Sémillon has a surprisingly low profile. In the northern hemisphere, it was traditionally not seen very much as an unblended varietal wine. This is largely because, in its native Bordeaux, it is always mixed with Sauvignon Blanc.

However, its highly prized susceptibility in the right conditions to botrytis, the so-called noble rot that concentrates the sugars of overripe grapes by shrivelling them on the vine, makes Sémillon a surefire bet as a dessert-wine producer. The lofty reputation enjoyed by sweet Sauternes and Barsac - in which Sémillon typically represents around four-fifths or more of the blend - has been such that the grape's role in the production of dry white wine has been largely eclipsed.

In Bordeaux today, producers of dry white wine are in the business of pulling out a lot of their Sémillon vines and replacing them with further plantings of its partner Sauvignon. (As we saw when we looked at Sauvignon Blanc, some of the trendiest dry whites of Bordeaux use no Sémillon at all.) That said, it still accounts for far more acreage in the vineyards than Sauvignon, so if it is in decline, the process will be a lengthy one. Many producers frankly consider it to have far less character than its brasher stablemate, being short of aromatic appeal and general *joie-de-vivre*.

To which one can only reply, tell that to the Australians. Semillon (as it is commonly spelt outside France) has been used to produce a varietal dry wine in southern Australia since the 19th century. Its homeland Down Under is the Hunter Valley in New South Wales. True, many growers weren't sure what the variety was, and its traditional (and misleading) name was Hunter Riesling. It does share some of the aromatic characteristics of real Riesling, most notably a minerally aroma of lime-zest, but it almost always gives a fatter, oilier wine than Riesling.

The most peculiar trait a dry Sémillon wine can have is to smell and taste as if it has been wood-matured when it hasn't. Often, there is a distinctly toasty quality to the wine that becomes steadily more pronounced as it ages. Its colour darkens rapidly too, making old Hunter Semillon one of the strangest but most memorable experiences in the world of white wine.

In areas where a lot of cheap bulk wine is produced, Sémillon's easy-going temperament in the vineyard has made it the grape of choice for those who haven't yet caught the Chardonnay bug. Much of South America's vineland, especially in Chile, is carpeted with the variety. An indication of the status in which it is held here is that these are not the wines Chile chooses to boast about on the export markets.

For many, Sémillon provides a relatively trouble-free source of blending material for more fashionable varieties. Although the Bordeaux precedent is to blend it with Sauvignon, Sauvignon is too much in vogue currently to be thought by many producers to need a partner in the bottle. That is why many winemakers, in Australia particularly, have taken to blending Semillon with Chardonnay.

The resulting wines have become bargain-basement alternatives to neat Chardonnay. The lowish prices of these wines indicate how seriously we are being asked to take them. In a hot vintage, where both grapes have yielded similarly rich, fat, silky-textured wines, it is difficult to see what they are supposed to be doing for each other in a blend.

On the other hand, the Sémillon-Sauvignon partnership is nearly always a happy one. The acidity of the latter gives definition to the textural opulence of the former.

The blend makes particular sense in the production of sweet wines. What makes great Sauternes, Barsac and Monbazillac so sought-after, and so extremely long-lived in the bottle, is that a good balance of sugar and acid is present in the wines to start with. Compared to lesser dessert wines from other wine regions, they are hardly ever cloying, despite their massive, syrupy concentration.

Sémillon, a golden-coloured grape with markedly deep green leaves (right) is often used to blend with Sauvignon or Chardonnay. When affected by botrytis (noble rot), it creates the world's finest dessert wines.

FRENCH ORIGINS
Bordeaux.

WHERE ELSE IS IT GROWN?
Australia, Chile, Argentina, a little in South Africa and California, and isolated pockets of southern France.

TASTING NOTES
When dry, lime-peel, exotic honey, sometimes has a little of Sauvignon's gooseberry too. Often has a hard mineral purity, even slightly metallic. In the Hunter Valley, deceptive woodiness even when unoaked, turning to burnt toast with age. Blended with Chardonnay, lemon-and-lime squash seems to be the main flavour. When subjected to botrytis for sweet wines, can take on a whole range of exotic fruit characters, but classically has overripe peach or apricot flavour, barley-sugar, honey, allied to a vanilla-custard, *crème brûlée* richness from oak ageing. Australian sweet Semillon can have an emphatically medicinal tinge to it as well.

Bordeaux

Sémillon grapes left on the vine that have been affected by botrytis (right). The shrivelled, blackened grapes will yield a lusciously sweet, concentrated juice.

Sémillon's most glorious display in its home region is in the wines of Sauternes and Barsac. At the top of the tree, with a classification to itself, is the legendary Château d'Yquem, the most expensive sweet wine in the world. The late-summer and autumn climate in Bordeaux provides perfect conditions in many years for the development on Sémillon of the noble rot, botrytis, that causes the berries to moulder and dry out on the vines. As the liquid proportion of the grapes drops, so the sugar in them comes to represent an ever higher percentage, and the result is lusciously sweet, alcoholic, sticky wines of enormous longevity.

If the top wines are so expensive, it is in large part because the more conscientious châteaux take great pains over the harvest. They will hand-select only those berries that are fully rotted, so labour costs are accordingly very high. Most of the wines are aged in at least a proportion of new oak, adding further dimensions of richness to them. These wines have for long been the inspiration for the production of botrytised Sémillon the world over.

The elegant Château La Louvière in Pessac-Léognan, Graves (below), owned by the Lurton family. Dry white Bordeaux from the Graves is often the best of its style.

Elsewhere in Bordeaux, in the making of dry wines, Sémillon rather hangs its head these days. The finger of blame for the old-style flabby, fruitless dry whites of the region has been pointed its way. But this style is on the wane as fresh young Sauvignon Blanc, with its tangier fruit flavours, shows it the door. As a result, consumers may get the idea that Sémillon is incapable of making great dry wine in Bordeaux, but it ain't necessarily so.

In the northern Graves region of Pessac-Léognan, close to the city, some of Bordeaux's most illustrious names in dry white wine production still use a greater percentage of Sémillon than Sauvignon Blanc in their wines. These include Châteaux Olivier, Laville-Haut-Brion and La Tour-Martillac.

New Zealand is beginning to have better success with Sémillon now that the particular strain (or clone) of the grape they had planted there is being replaced with better ones. For the time being, it is best in the Bordeaux-blend style, as exemplified by the oak-fermented Sauvignon-Semillon of North Island producer Selaks.

Australia

Dry Semillon is one of a handful of unique styles of wine that Australia has contributed to the world. Nor is it a product of some antipodean search for novelty, conceived in a struggle to find ways of doing things that escape the eternal French archetypes. Australia was making Semillons like this in the late 19th century, even though it may have been calling them Hunter Riesling or - even less convincingly - White Burgundy.

The classic Hunter Valley style can be quite austere, as typified by the wines of Tyrrells. Crisp and acerbic in youth, they age to a wonderful roasted-nuts complexity, all achieved without recourse to the expense of oak barrels. Some producers do actually use a modicum of oak to emphasise that natural toastiness. With the tendency now for consumers to drink most wines young, greater stress is being laid on primary fruit flavours - sharp green fruits, usually lime, being the main reference point. Other good Hunter producers are Rothbury, Brokenwood and Lindeman's.

The grape pops up in most Australian regions, though, and fares equally well in areas that are considerably cooler than the Hunter. In the Clare Valley, for instance, Semillon produces a less oily version. As a rough guide, producers who make good Riesling are likely to be reliable for Semillon too: in a cool part of the Clare called Lenswood, Tim Knappstein makes fine, bracingly tart but certainly ageworthy wines.

Western Australia's Margaret River region makes some generously fruity, distinctly smoky Semillons in a style hugely reminiscent of Sauvignon. Evans & Tate is a prime example here.

Although unblended Sauvignon can too often be a disappointment from many parts of Australia, when it is blended with Semillon in the Bordeaux fashion it can produce impressively ripe-fruited wines capable of gaining real complexity with ageing. Cape Mentelle in Margaret River and even St Hallett, in the broiling Barossa Valley region of South Australia, make good blends.

Botrytised, or noble-rotted, Semillon has a long and distinguished tradition here, too. The style may be big and obvious when compared with the top wines of Sauternes, but then there is no particular reason to compare them to Sauternes. De Bortoli in New South Wales was among those who blazed this particular trail, while Peter Lehmann makes a textbook orange-barley-sugar version in the Barossa.

The de Bortoli winery in New South Wales, Australia (below), complete with irrigation canal.

The verdant landscape of South Australia's Clare Valley (below), with Lenswood Vineyard in the foreground. A cool upland district, it can produce bracingly tart but ageworthy Semillons.

SYRAH

Whether recognised as the French grape of the northern Rhône, Syrah, or in its popular guise as Shiraz, in Australia, this grape remains one of the noblest red varieties, fabled for its ability to age majestically for decades.

SUCH IS the success of this grape in Australia that many may know it only by its southern-hemisphere name of Shiraz. More of it is grown there than any other red wine grape, and it appears in the bottle either alone or in the company of Cabernet Sauvignon - a highly successful partnership for which there is no French precedent.

Although a fair amount of Shiraz is of no more than ordinary, every-day quality, it is without doubt among the first division of international grape varieties, as witness the fact that the most fabled red wine of Australia - Penfold's Grange - is overwhelmingly composed of Shiraz, with the merest dash of Cabernet to season it.

Shiraz produces some of the world's deepest, darkest, most intense red wines, full of liquorice richness, hot spice and alcoholic power. Then again, it can be used to make the kind of sweetly jammy, oak-smoothed nursery wine that can lure confirmed white wine drinkers on to red once in a while.

As Syrah, as we should call it when in France, it blends well with a number of other grapes, and hangs around with a very mixed gang of rough diamonds and ne'er-do-wells in the wines of the southern Rhône and Languedoc-Roussillon.

The Rhône valley is the ancestral home of Syrah. In viticultural terms, the valley divides into two zones - northern and southern - and represents two very different approaches to the grape. In the south, it makes its way among a large coterie of minor varieties, from the rough-and-ready reds of Côtes du Rhône and Côtes du Ventoux up to the twin stars of Châteauneuf-du-Pape and Gigondas.

Producers of red Châteauneuf may choose from a menu of no fewer than 13 grapes (although hardly anybody uses all of them), of which Syrah may play only second or third fiddle. The northern Rhône is where Syrah really comes into its own.

The vibrant blue of the Syrah grape variety (right). Syrah has a unique character most often described as "peppery", and responds well to oak. In its classic form as the grape of northern Rhône's finest reds, and in Australia as Shiraz, it can make wines that will age for decades.

Hermitage is the most celebrated wine of the north; like the other northern appellations, its reds must be constituted from 100 per cent Syrah. (The one exception to that is Côte-Rôtie, where the wine may idiosyncratically contain up to 20 per cent of the white variety Viognier, although by no means all the growers use it.)

These monumental, classic reds can age for at least as long as the very greatest Bordeaux, on account of their precise and complex balances of hugely concentrated fruit, acidity and massive extract. Generally, they are not remotely approachable until around six or seven years old, and the best need perhaps twice as long as that to begin to uncoil into the exotically seductive beauties they can be.

At the most accessible end of the scale, and not to be confused with Hermitage itself, is Crozes-Hermitage, whose wines can be drinkable at a mere three or four years old. They may not be anything like as dazzling as the best Hermitage and Côte-Rôtie but, across the board, they do offer a genuine insight into the unique flavours of Syrah.

One of the most commonly encountered descriptions of Syrah wines is "peppery", and even a simple Crozes from a co-operative can display something of that characteristic, although it may vary in intensity from a mild suggestion of spiciness at the back of the throat to the exact and inescapable smell of freshly milled black peppercorns, as if the winemaker had given the wine a few twists of the grinder before bottling it.

In Australian Shiraz, that pepperiness is distinctly more muted. The fruit flavours are generally riper and more obvious, and the wines rarely have that sharp edge of tannin that northern Rhône examples do. In youth, the softer contours of Shiraz are derived from the overt influence of creamy oak flavours, so that the wine can be drunk sooner than can Syrah.

The stylistic differences between the French and Australian manifestations of the grape are therefore comparable to those of Cabernet Sauvignon. From some regions, especially South Australia's Barossa Valley, Shiraz can

FRENCH ORIGINS
Northern Rhône.

WHERE ELSE IS IT GROWN?
Australia. A little in California
and South Africa. Is of some
significance in Switzerland.

TASTING NOTES
Can smell of almost any dark
purple fruit - blackberries,
blackcurrants, black cherries,
damsons, plums. Freshly ground
black pepper in the northern
Rhône. Exotic flavours can
include liquorice, ginger, dark
chocolate, often a distinct floral
note, too, like violets. Cool
topnote of mint characteristic in
parts of South Australia.
Aged wines can take on
something of the gaminess of
old Pinot Noir.

take on a surprisingly delicate aromatic range,
so that the leather and tar and pepper the grape
traditionally rejoices in may be overlaid with a
refreshing waft of eucalyptus.

Australians have also used some of their Shiraz to make a thoroughly innovative thick red
sparkling wine that tastes of frothing blackcurrant juice - a quickly acquired taste to most who
come across it. Those whose vinous memories
go back to fizzy red Lambrusco should abandon
their trepidation: sparkling Shiraz is a hedon-
istic mouthful of purple southern sunshine.

France

The greatest names in Rhône Syrah are now ranked up with Bordeaux's and Burgundy's finest. It is still a very recent phenomenon, though. While the burly red wines of Hermitage had always had a lofty reputation among British wine connoisseurs, the production of the region as a whole was not held in particularly high regard. When the esteemed American wine critic Robert Parker began, in the 1980s, to rate some of the best wines of Marcel Guigal (one of the northern Rhône's superstars) as the equals of great vintages of Mouton-Rothschild, the international wine trade was persuaded to take notice.

The chapel and vines on the famous hill of Hermitage (below), overlooking the river Rhône and the towns of Tournon and Tain l'Hermitage.

That development inevitably allowed the producers to put up their prices, but it has to be said that the best had certainly been undervalued in the past. These are wines with the same sort of structure and ageing capacity as Cabernet-based clarets (often even more muscularly built, in fact) and their flavours resemble no other red wines in France.

Of the northern Rhône appellations for varietal Syrah, Hermitage is traditionally the biggest and beefiest. Although solidly constructed, the wines are not without grace and elegance, and the fruit flavour can be surprisingly lighter than the norm - more raspberries than blackberries. Chave is a fine producer, while the Hermitage La Chapelle of Jaboulet, whose wines crop up all over the Rhône, is a densely textured, ferociously dark stunner.

Côte-Rôtie is the appellation that has created all the excitement in recent years. Guigal's top three wines from single vineyards (La Mouline, La Landonne and La Turque) are mind-blowingly concentrated expressions of pure Syrah that sell for sky-high prices, but there are other growers such as Jamet, Delas and Vidal-Fleury whose formidable talents have helped shore up the reputation of this area.

St-Joseph makes slightly lighter wines, with piercingly ripe fruit in the good years, while the bottom-line appellation of Crozes-Hermitage is well worth trying as an introduction to the flavours of Rhône Syrah. (A stunning exception is the Crozes of a grower called Graillot, whose wines are as opaquely black and intense as some Hermitage.)

The final appellation of the northern Rhône, Cornas, is an odd one; its Syrah is the least immediately recognisable. The wines are often rather tough without the benefit of youthful fruit, or they can simply taste more like blended wines from areas further south like Châteauneuf-du-Pape. That said, Colombo, Clape and Voge are three of the better producers making some exciting Syrahs in Cornas.

In the southern Rhône, and down into Languedoc, Syrah is blended with many other red grapes, the most important of which is Grenache, which we shall meet shortly. Unless a producer has used a particularly high percentage of Syrah, the grape may not be individually perceptible in these wines.

Australia

Shiraz has been *the* pre-eminent red grape variety in Australia for as long as anyone can remember, but it is only in the last 20 years or so that there has been a significant impetus towards producing world-class wine from it. At its most humdrum, Shiraz is a rather gloopy plum-jam sort of wine with too much heavy oak flavour in it, so that the toffee sweetness of its aftertaste can quickly become cloying. Thankfully, there are more than enough accomplished Shiraz producers to make for a brighter picture.

It's all a question, as so often, of microclimate. In the hotter parts of the country, such as the Hunter and Barossa valleys, Shiraz is responsible for the thickest, most opulently fruity of all Australia's reds. Charles Melton and St Hallett Old Block Shiraz (so-called because it is made from a particularly venerable plot of vines) are emblematic of the Barossa

style; Rothbury offers a leaner, but still intensely aromatic Hunter Valley alternative. In the hotter northeast corner of Victoria, the Goulburn Valley is home to some especially concentrated Shirazes, notably from Chateau Tahbilk.

The red soil of Coonawarra is as distinguished a hotbed of Shiraz as it is of Cabernet Sauvignon. The Penfold's range of reds draws extensively on plantings in this area, as do the subtly spiced Shiraz-based wines of the Penley Estate and the accessibly fruit-filled offerings of Wynns, not all of which use oak.

Along with Penfold's Grange, one of the most majestic of all Australian Shiraz wines comes from the Henschke winery's Hill of Grace vineyard in the Barossa. The vines planted here are over a century old, and produce small amounts of extraordinarily deep, resonant and complex wine that lasts for years.

The Hill of Grace vineyard, owned by Henschke (above), in the Barossa Valley, South Australia. The Shiraz vines planted here are over 100 years old.

Other Regions

SOUTH AFRICA
As in Australia, it took a while for Shiraz to persuade its growers that it was worth taking seriously as a grape variety. Inspired by success elsewhere, however, some impressive Shiraz is now beginning to emerge from the Cape. It should work, after all, given that most of South Africa's wine regions enjoy just the sort of sultry climatic conditions that Shiraz loves. Hartenberg in Stellenbosch and Fairview in Paarl are just a couple of the more conspicuously successful Shiraz producers to date.

CALIFORNIA
Despite the fashion in recent years on the West Coast for Rhône grape varieties, Syrah - as it tends to be known in the United States - has not really established itself as a particularly important grape. The trend so far has been to make a wine with French levels of acidity and memorably aromatic fruit, but not quite the degree of extract of the most well-bred Hermitage and Côte-Rôtie. Two wineries setting the pace have been Qupé in Santa Barbara and Joseph Phelps in the Napa Valley.

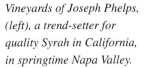

Orderly rows of Shiraz vines at Franschhoek's Bellingham Vineyards, Paarl, South Africa (above).

Vineyards of Joseph Phelps, (left), a trend-setter for quality Syrah in California, in springtime Napa Valley.

RIESLING

Germany's noble white grape variety, Riesling, is a versatile performer. It is prized in northern Europe and the southern hemisphere for its ability to produce classic sweet whites as well as impeccable dry wines.

The Riesling (right) is a hardy, frost-resistant vine, which makes it ideal for the cool vineyards of northern Europe. Riesling can produce long-lived wines of intense aroma and character, ranging in style from bone-dry to lusciously sweet.

THE ONLY FINE wine grape of international importance not to have originated in France, Riesling is the great speciality of German winemaking. Its only base in France is in the Alsace region, a sheltered northeastern enclave between the Vosges mountains and the Rhine valley that was a geo-political part of Germany for much of its history. Like the Sémillon we looked at earlier, Riesling is capable of making impeccably dry wines of surprising longevity, as well as lusciously sweet dessert wines affected by the noble rot, botrytis, but unlike Sémillon it also runs the whole gamut of styles in between.

In recent years, Riesling has come to be considered the most underrated of all the top grapes. Why this should be so when it is such a versatile performer might seem a mystery until one bears in mind the baleful influence of a certain sweet wine produced in huge quantities, and which wrongly came to be seen as virtually synonymous with the whole German wine industry. No matter that there is no mention of Riesling on labels of branded Liebfraumilch (although most brands do actually contain an insignificant proportion) - Liebfraumilch was German, and so was Riesling.

The great problem German wines have to overcome is that nearly all wine drinkers - except those who grow up within spitting distance of a vineyard and are weaned on the local wine - cut their teeth on products like Liebfraumilch. It's sweet, it's not noticeably alcoholic and it doesn't seem to contain the tart acids that drier white wines have. When tastes become more sophisticated, meaning drier, an important part of the rite of passage for the budding wine enthusiast is to shun such wines as "kids' stuff", and the more serious German wines get swept aside in that process.

If only Liebfraumilch had its own peculiar bottle. But it sits proudly on retail shelves next to top-quality Rhine Rieslings in identically tall, narrow flute bottles of dark brown glass (wines from the northerly Mosel valley, where Liebfraumilch may not be made, are bottled in similarly shaped green glass). Attempts to persuade customers to look for the word "Riesling" on the label amid the thicket of polysyllabic Gothic lettering may still run aground on the fact that, even when newcomers do try these wines, the twin qualities they dismiss in the cheap branded wines are still there more often than not: lightness and some degree of sweetness.

Because Germany's vineyards are at the northern extremity of where vines can be grown and still produce crops of fermentable fruit, its quality classification system developed along the lines of assessing just how ripe the grapes were when harvested and therefore how potentially sweet the resulting wine would be.

Historically, before it was feasible to maintain stable conditions in the winery, the severely low temperatures of the northern winter would bring the fermentation to a halt. This would leave plenty of natural sugar (as opposed to an added sweetener, as in Liebfraumilch) in what was a low-alcohol wine. Up until the early years of this century, this was precisely the style that connoisseurs prized above all in German wines. Many consider these are still Germany's greatest claims to fame today.

Driven by international taste trends, a movement gathered pace in Germany in the 1980s and '90s to ferment the wines - Rieslings and others - all the way out to dryness, resulting in bone-dry wine that reached the kind of alcohol level (around 12 per cent) that white wine drinkers were more familiar with. The experiment ended in tears for some, as consumers rejected the searingly acidic, sour-grapefruit flavours these wines possessed. The compromise style was *Halbtrocken* - half-dry, or off-dry.

Riesling always gives a high-acid wine, which is perhaps best balanced in Germany by some level of natural sweetness, so that even those at the lower end of the classification have a softening edge on them, akin to sprinkling a grapefruit with at least a pinch of sugar. In warmer climes, there is enough ripeness and

ORIGINS
Germany.

WHERE ELSE IS IT GROWN?
Alsace. Australia and New Zealand. Austria and northern Italy. Some in the United States and Canada.

TASTING NOTES
Nearly always has both the scent and taste of fresh lime, whether bitter zests or sweetened juice. Riper German ones can have softer fruit like ripe peach or apricot, as well as a gentle floral aroma. In Alsace, there is a very austere mineral quality in the wines and a texture on the palate like sharpened steel. The whiff of petrol (or gasoline) flowing from the pump generally comes with age, although some Australian wines can display it quite young.

alcohol to offset the high acidity, so that the wines feel perfectly balanced when fully dry.

This is the case in both Alsace and Australia, where the vine is as highly prized as it is in Germany. One useful attribute of pronounced acidity is ageing potential, and even the lightest German Rieslings have the capacity to keep well and improve for many years, their first flush of tart citric fruit turning into an extraordinary, and powerfully spellbinding, pungency that has classically (and accurately) been compared to the heady fume of petrol before combustion.

Germany

Riesling is grown in nearly all of the wine regions of Germany, although it is by no means the most widely planted variety. It is in many ways particularly well suited to the cold climates it encounters there, because the tough stems of its vines enable them to cope with the worst the winters can throw at them.

The drawback comes at the other end of the annual cycle, when ripening the grapes is something of a gamble against the elements. Picked too early, Riesling can be full of hard, unripe acidity. Waiting for the right levels of ripeness can often mean leaving the bunches hanging into November, when French growers have long since picked, pressed and fermented, and when the weather is so bitter that it can be hard to get a natural fermentation going.

With all that in mind, much effort and funding has gone into crossing Riesling with other German varieties, or producing crosses with no Riesling in them, and then crossing the crosses with Riesling and others. The aim has been to try to perfect a grape that will give the fresh fruit flavours of Riesling, as well as its invaluable susceptibility to botrytis, but with a more reliable ripening pattern. A handful of these have yielded goodish results, but no one seriously believes they can take the place of Riesling as Germany's premier performer.

The top classification for German wines, their equivalent of the French *appellation contrôlée*, is *Qualitätswein mit Prädikat* or QmP (literally quality wine with distinction). Within this class, there are five types of wine, measured according to the amount of sweetness in them. In ascending order, they are: *Kabinett, Spätlese, Auslese, Beerenauslese* and *Trockenbeerenauslese*. The "-lese" means "picked", and the time of picking is indicated in the prefix, from Spätlese (late-picked, ie. just after the normal harvesting time) to Trockenbeerenauslese or TBA (meaning berries picked outside or after the main harvest that are dried and shrivelled with sugar-concentrating rot).

The famous steep vineyards of the Mosel region (below) where the Riesling vines tumble down towards the Mosel river. Such steep sites means hand-picking is the only option at harvest-time.

Any of the first three styles may be fermented out to total dryness to become Trocken (dry) wines, or halfway in the case of Halbtrocken. Some super-sweet berries are left on the vines until nearer Christmas, in some vintages even into the New Year, and are picked at the crack of dawn when they are frozen solid. During the pressing, some of the crystals of ice that represent the water content of the grapes are removed and the very sweet juice that hasn't frozen is then fermented. This style is known, for obvious reasons, as *Eiswein*.

The fullest, most concentrated Rieslings have traditionally come from the Rheingau, where there is more of this grape planted than any of Germany's other varieties. It is also where the best producers make wines that are as expressive of their particular vineyard locations as any Burgundy *grand cru*.

History insists that the Rheingau was the region where the first noble-rotted wines were accidentally produced, years before the technique was exported to Sauternes. A non-Trocken Riesling from the Rheingau is generally around 10 per cent alcohol, quite heady in German terms, and

there is a rounded, often honeyed feel to the best of them. Leading estates are Schloss Johannisberg, Balthasar Ress and Robert Weil.

To the west of the Rheingau, the Nahe also has a preponderance of Riesling, although here it is a more recent development as a result of the region's standing having risen considerably in the last few years. Anheuser is one of the growers' names on everybody's lips.

The other two neighbouring Rhine regions are Rheinhessen and Pfalz (the latter originally known in English as the Palatinate). Riesling has made great strides in the Pfalz. The stars of the show are the wines of Müller-Catoir, where an almost tropical intensity is the house style. Lingenfelder's offerings are in the more delicate, traditional style, but quite as accomplished.

To the northwest, and centred on the city of Trier, the Mosel-Saar-Ruwer region produces the lightest, most exquisitely subtle and refined versions of Riesling anywhere in the world. Alcohol levels may be as low as 7 per cent, and the aromatic profile of the wines so astonishingly rarefied that a sniff at the glass can be like breathing in pure mountain air. The vineyards are planted on vertiginously steep slopes on either side of the river, so any thought of harvesting by machines is out of the question. Fritz Haag, Dr. Loosen and J. J. Prüm are among the finest winemakers of the Mosel.

Vineyards looking down to the village of Ungstein, in the Pfalz region of Germany (above). The traditional style of Riesling wines here is both aromatic and tremendously delicate.

Schloss Johannisberg, looking down over its Riesling vineyards (left), in the Rheingau. Rheingau Rieslings are traditionally the fullest, most concentrated in style.

Alsace

The 15th-century church in the midst of vineyards at Hunawihr, Alsace (above).

Those familiar with the wines of Alsace may tend more readily to associate them with the highly perfumed, positively decadent flavours of Gewurztraminer and Pinot Gris than with the steely austerity of Riesling. It is, however, an open secret in the region that Riesling is considered the noblest of them all, partly because the acidity levels it usually attains mean that the resulting wines have a good long life ahead of them. About a fifth of all Alsace vineyard land is planted with this variety, and the total is steadily mounting.

It is in the hilly Haut-Rhin district of Alsace that most of the Riesling is concentrated. The best plots are those that are protected from the wind so that the ripening of the grape is not inhibited, although the climate of this particularly sheltered region is much more benign than German growers have to contend with. Unusually for a fine wine grape, the amount of fruit the vines are permitted to yield under the appellation regulations is quite high, without the wines themselves necessarily lacking anything in intensity.

Most Alsace Riesling is made in an assertively bone-dry style, with quite powerful alcohol and rapier-like acidity. They are the only Alsace wines that are not especially enjoyable if drunk young, most requiring at least five years to begin to settle down. In their youth, they have a highly strung, quite taut feel on the palate, leavened with some bracing citric fruit, comparable to freshly squeezed lime juice.

In addition to the basic dry wines, there are two designations for sweeter styles. The lighter of the two is *Vendange Tardive* (meaning late harvest); in a warm, late summer the grapes are left on the vines to achieve higher sugar levels that convert to a delicately sweet wine. If conditions are right, ie. damp misty mornings giving way to mild sunny daytime weather, Riesling will botrytise, just as it does in Germany. The hugely concentrated syrupy wines that result are called *Sélection de Grains Nobles* - among the most appealingly balanced nobly-rotted dessert wines in all of France.

Certain of the best vineyard sites in Alsace have been designated *grands crus* since the mid-1980s. Only four of the grapes permitted in Alsace, Riesling included, may be planted in these areas. The wines should have a noticeable extra dimension of intensity in the flavour, and are inevitably sold for higher prices.

Among the foremost producers of Alsace Riesling are Zind-Humbrecht, Hugel, Schlumberger, Trimbach and Louis Sipp.

Steeply shelving vineyards form the backdrop to the typically alsacien architecture of Trimbach's premises at Ribeauvillé, Alsace (right).

Other Regions

AUSTRALIA

There was once more Riesling in Australia than there was Chardonnay, which may come as a sobering thought to a wine world obsessed with the sun-drenched oaky flavours of Aussie Chardonnay. Because it needs a certain amount of acidity in order to define its flavours, the variety is much more successful in the cooler areas of the country, such as the Clare Valley of South Australia and parts of Western Australia such as Mount Barker.

The Australian style is richer and fatter than the European models. In youth, they have pungent lemon-and-lime fruit and oily texture. Sometimes, most notably in wines from Clare Valley, they also display those heady petrol fumes that German and Alsace Rieslings only tend to take on with bottle-age. Despite their smoother angles, the most sensitively made Australian Rieslings still show good acid balance to maintain that sense of freshness without which Riesling wines are lost.

Because they used to call their Semillon grapes Hunter Riesling, there was once a risk of some confusion in Australian consumers' minds about the identity of the true Riesling. This is why some of the wines are still labelled Rhine Riesling, but that doesn't mean to say that those labelled simply "Riesling" are not the real thing: they are.

Among the top producers of Australian Riesling are Tim Knappstein, Tim Adams, Petaluma, Hill-Smith and Frankland Estate.

NEW ZEALAND

Across the Tasman Sea, New Zealand's cooler climes should be ideally suited to the production of good dry Riesling. In fact, there was a tendency until fairly recently to make an indeterminate medium-dry sort of wine. The South Island has since led the way in producing fresh, clean, impeccably lime-flavoured Rieslings of great promise. Redwood Valley in Nelson and Wairarapa's Martinborough Vineyards, in the north of South Island, are two of the outstanding examples. When vintage conditions permit, many producers also make a botrytised Riesling (as they do in Australia).

UNITED STATES

Cooler parts of California and particularly Washington State have seen tentative plantings of Riesling, but it is fair to say the grape has not so far proved the hottest property commercially in the USA. The Kiona winery in Washington makes an excellent late-picked Riesling. Further north, in Canada, Riesling is turning out some convincing wines in the province of Ontario. Some of Canada's fabled Ice Wines use Riesling; the top ones can challenge the best of German Eiswein.

Harvesting Riesling grapes in the depths of winter, (above) in Ontario, Canada. The frozen grapes are destined for Canada's fabled Ice Wine.

Checking the progress of bunches of ripening Riesling (left), in South Australia's Clare Valley, one of the grape's best growing areas.

MERLOT

Historically used in the blended reds of Bordeaux, Merlot's fame is founded on its partnership with Cabernet Sauvignon. Its reputation as a solo performer has been earned more recently.

FOR WINEMAKERS all over the world, Merlot is the significant other of Cabernet Sauvignon, its best blending friend and truest partner. Whereas Cabernet, rightly or wrongly, came to be seen as capable of performing in its own right, Merlot was not generally thought to have the wherewithal to produce great things alone - at least not at first.

Merlot may have been used alone for industrial quantities of everyday quaffing wine in the northern half of Italy, but in its homeland of Bordeaux, where it made its name, the red wines are always blended.

In Bordeaux, Merlot is considered very much the junior partner. This is because the five levels of *crus classés* that constitute Bordeaux's aristocracy are concentrated on the left bank - the Cabernet Sauvignon side - of the Gironde, in Médoc (and at Château Haut-Brion, lower down in Cabernet-dominated Graves). In fact, there is far more Merlot planted than there is Cabernet, largely because it plays a significant part in the red wines made in the less illustrious parts of the region.

But Merlot does have a starring role to play in Bordeaux, in the two best areas of the right bank, Pomerol and St-Emilion. Although Pomerol and St-Emilion were both left out of the celebrated 1855 classification that created the *crus classés*, they too have their famous names and their own individual styles. Some Pomerol properties use virtually all Merlot in their reds; the leader of the pack, Château Pétrus, is all Merlot down to the last five per cent, which is accounted for by the less widespread Cabernet Franc. Since no red wine in Bordeaux commands anything like the stratospheric price of Pétrus, it is clear that Merlot has no need to hide its light under a bushel of Cabernet Sauvignon.

In fact, as in most regions where the foremost wines are blends of two or more grape varieties, Bordeaux growers mix and match their propor-

The plump, blue Merlot (right), an early-ripening grape, produces soft, rich wines - often described as "fleshy" - that harmonise well with the more structured Cabernet Sauvignon.

tions of Cabernet, Merlot and the others, according to what nature has bequeathed them that year in the way of vintage conditions. Merlot tends to ripen a little earlier than Cabernet, so if late rain or a sudden cool snap at the end of the growing season spoils the chances of great Cabernet, at least there may have been some good-quality Merlot to draw on.

Even in the better years, Merlot can often produce healthier, more concentrated grapes than its colleague, the fine vintage of 1990 being a recent example.

Stylistically, what Merlot does for Cabernet in the wines of the Médoc is to smooth away some of its harder edges. Since Merlot is a thinner-skinned variety than Cabernet, it produces a less tannic wine, thus mitigating some of the astringency of prickly young Cabernet. (It may also, for the same reason, lighten the colour of the wine.) A claret that uses, say, 35 per cent Merlot will have a noticeably softer feel than one where it is limited to a mere 10 per cent.

Outside Bordeaux, Merlot really started to branch out on its own during the 1980s in California. Varietal Merlot had been produced in California before this, but the tendency was towards inky, fierce and tannic wines - not a mode that Merlot takes to particularly well. In the latter half of the '80s, the style began to change and a kinder, gentler Merlot emerged that has found great favour with consumers

looking for a softer type of red for everyday drinking. West Coast Merlot-mania is such that plantings of the grape in California increased fivefold in the decade from the mid-'80s to the mid-'90s, and are still on the increase.

Growers in Washington State have also discovered that their climate is rather good at producing the kind of concentrated but velvet-soft red that newcomers to red wine especially appreciate. In the USA, at least, Merlot is a grape whose time has come.

In the southern hemisphere, it is only lately beginning to gain ground in the same way. Argentina has a fair amount of Merlot planted, and more Chilean winemakers are now producing it as a varietal wine. In Australia and New Zealand, it has so far been seen mainly as a blending partner for Cabernet à la Bordeaux, but there are signs that solo Merlot is finding its feet.

FRENCH ORIGINS
Bordeaux, especially the Libournais on the right bank of the Gironde, which includes St-Emilion and Pomerol.

WHERE ELSE IS IT GROWN?
Throughout central and eastern Europe, from Switzerland to Bulgaria. United States. Argentina. Some in Chile, Australia, New Zealand, South Africa.

TASTING NOTES
At its ripest, soft purple fruits such as blackberries and black plums. In cooler climates, it can have a distinct vegetal streak in it, like green beans or asparagus. If the sun gets to it, there may be a suggestion of dried fruit such as raisins or even fruitcake. Rounded out with oak in the best wines of Pomerol and California, it can also take on a textural richness that has overtones of melted chocolate or possibly Turkish Delight.

France

The fairy-tale Château Ausone (above), in St-Emilion, set amid its vines.

The legendary Château Pétrus, Pomerol (below). Oil burners are still used in the vineyards as late as May to protect the early-ripening Merlot from frost damage.

Merlot's French fiefdom is on the right bank in Bordeaux. There it dominates the communes of Pomerol and St-Emilion. While red wines from the latter district are characteristically composed of around two-thirds Merlot with perhaps just a splash of Cabernet Sauvignon, in Pomerol the percentage may be more like nine-tenths Merlot, with no Cabernet Sauvignon at all.

Differences in character between the two communes are fairly subtle, but the top wines of Pomerol tend to have a seriousness and austerity about them, together with something of the dry, herbal flavour found in left-bank Cabernet. St-Emilion wines, on the other hand, for all that there may be less Merlot in them, are often softer and more approachable in their youth. Despite the popular assumption that Merlot-based wines mature more quickly than those dominated by Cabernet Sauvignon, St-Emilions and Pomerols can be quite as long-lived as the finest offerings of the Médoc.

In 1955, on the 100th anniversary of the Bordeaux classification system, St-Emilion endowed itself with a similar league table of quality. In contrast to the entrenched immutability of the left bank, however, the proprietors of St-Emilion undertook to update their classification every ten years. There may be little change from decade to decade, but perhaps that is precisely because they know their wines will be rigorously re-assessed, and so the motivation to maintain standards is acutely compelling. Top spot is shared deservedly by two châteaux: Cheval Blanc and Ausone.

Alone among the premier communes of Bordeaux, Pomerol has never been subjected to the trials of classification, and there are no plans to do so. After the legendary Pétrus, its other high-performance names include Châteaux le Gay, Trotanoy, l'Evangile, le Bon Pasteur, Vieux-Château-Certan and Clos l'Eglise.

Less illustrious Merlot-based wines come from the "satellite" areas of St-Emilion, a group of small communes that form a northeasterly fringe to St-Emilion itself and are all allowed to append its name to their own - Montagne, Lussac, Puisseguin, St-Georges. In good vintages, when the grander properties can fetch dizzyingly high prices for their wines, some of these satellite wines can represent exemplary value. Bel-Air, in Puisseguin, and Lyonnat, in Lussac, are but two good examples.

Elsewhere, Merlot has made great inroads among the varietal wines being produced in the Languedoc under the catch-all Vin de Pays d'Oc designation, and it also has a part to play in some of the traditional appellations of the southwest. In Cahors, for example, it performs its time-honoured role, tempering the sterner attributes of the Auxerrois and Tannat grapes.

Rest of the World

UNITED STATES

Merlot is the red wine of choice for those California and Washington wine-drinkers who want the richness and structure of a good red, without having to age it until it is soft enough to drink. In that respect, it's very much Cabernet without tears. For once, fashion has proven a beneficial influence, because the Merlot craze has led many winemakers to look again at the most suitable ways of vinifying the grape. The benchmark style is now ripe red fruit with a lick of sweet oak and gentle tannins.

Good Merlots come from Duckhorn, Murphy-Goode, Ravenswood and Newton in California, and Chateau Ste Michelle and Hogue Cellars in Washington State.

Merlot is the most widely planted red grape variety in Romania (left), making soft, easy-drinking reds.

ITALY

It's fair to say that Merlot does not enjoy a particularly exalted reputation in Italy, although large swathes of its wine industry - especially in the northeastern areas of the Veneto, Friuli and Piave - would be lost without it. The tendency is to make a light-toned, juicy red from it, such as the classic lunchtime thirst-quenchers served by the carafe in *trattorie*. In hotter years and from producers prepared to limit their yields, however, there can be a little meaty complexity to the wines.

In the hotbed of viticultural experimentation that is Tuscany, one or two of the smart operators are achieving fine results with Merlot. Producers such as Lodovico Antinori, with his varietal Merlot, Masseto, are showing that the variety can make full-blooded, age-worthy wines that are the equals of the monumental Cabernet and Sangiovese super-Tuscans that attracted all the attention in the 1980s.

SOUTHERN HEMISPHERE

Australia and New Zealand are only really starting out in the varietal Merlot stakes. The custom has been to blend it with Cabernet, although in Australia Shiraz is, as we have seen, the preferred partner to Cabernet. Delegats and Corbans are among those producing New Zealand's more characterful showings.

In South Africa again, the grape is mostly seen as a constituent of the classic Bordeaux blend, but the Fairview, Glen Carlou and Zonnebloem estates have all produced good varietal Merlots.

The grape is gaining ground similarly in South America, particularly in Argentina, where it occupies the same extent of vineyard area as Cabernet. The small quantity of Chilean Merlot has included some wines of stunning potential, most notably that of the Valdivieso winery.

EASTERN EUROPE

Merlot was one of the mainstays of the Bulgarian wine revolution, and Reserve bottlings of it were (and are) often more pleasingly balanced wines than that country's Cabernets. In Romania, it turns out to be the most widely planted red grape, where it is responsible for many good, soft reds at keenly competitive prices.

Barrel cellars at Lodovico Antinori (below), Tuscany. Antinori is one of the band of top Tuscan producers creating stunning varietal Merlots.

CHENIN BLANC

Chenin Blanc's wide stylistic repertoire has made it the focal grape variety in the central vineyards of the Loire valley. Put through its paces in Vouvray, it runs the gamut of dry to sweet, and sparkling, wines.

PERHAPS THE most misunderstood of all the noble grape varieties, Chenin Blanc is the backbone of white winemaking in the Loire valley. While it undoubtedly has a very distinct and instantly recognisable profile in the wines it can produce, it has experienced difficulties in making friends among consumers for at least two reasons.

One is that, like Riesling, it has a wide stylistic repertoire, ranging all the way from the uncompromisingly bone-dry to luxurious botrytised dessert wines with decades of ageing potential. Nothing wrong with that, except that, in the past, the labelling on Chenin wines from the Loire has been low on information about the style of the wine.

The other hurdle for newcomers to clear is that the drier wines are not over-endowed with the sort of immediately obvious commercial appeal found in crisp, young fruit-filled Sauvignon Blanc. There is an aromatic character to Chenin, but after an initial burst of youthful fruit it turns into something quite different: a strange mixture of polished steel, old honey and damp. The classic tasting description often heard is "wet wool". Add to that the fact that Chenin is nearly always loaded with teeth-grinding acidity, and it is easier to understand why this is not a grape likely to be top of anyone's list of all-time favourites.

Learning to appreciate Chenin requires a slightly more precise knowledge of when to drink the different styles of wines than is the case with most other white wine varieties.

In the Loire, Vouvray is the most important appellation for Chenin. Its wines span the spectrum from dry to sweet, as well as a sparkling wine made by the champagne-method. The dry wines, increasingly labelled *sec* these days, can be delicious immediately on release, when they can display exhilarating fruit flavours, and that boldly assertive acid acts as a seasoning in the way that lemon juice does in a fruit purée. After a year, they seem to lose that fruit and slump into a prolonged sulk; tasted again at five or six years old, they have developed a honeyed softness that throws that dryness into relief.

In a hotter vintage, the winemaker may choose to leave some of the ripe natural sugars of the grape in the finished wine. This off-dry or medium-dry style is usually labelled *demi-sec*. It can be the most supremely refreshing example of its kind to be found anywhere in France. The delicate note of lingering sweetness tenderises the prickly acids in a hugely appetising way.

If the grapes reach a level of sticky-sweet overripeness that the French call *surmaturité*, then the resulting wine is known as *moelleux*. These are not quite the richest dessert wines - they still have that spiky streak of acidity running through the middle of them - but they do have a good coating of honey and caramel.

In years when botrytis has freely developed, some producers may make a fully botrytised wine. This will often be entitled *Sélection* because it involves selecting only the most extensively shrivelled berries from the vine, for maximum impact. Even then, the layers of concentrated sweetness have a discernible tartness at the centre, so that the overall effect is more toffee-apple than *crème brûlée*.

Elsewhere in the world, Chenin's malleability has made it something of a workhorse grape. That is certainly the case in the hotter regions of the United States and Australia, where its most widespread use has been as blending fodder, to add a tingle of acid and prevent basic white wines from tasting flabby. It is very extensively planted in South Africa, where it more often than not goes under the alias of Steen. While a lot of it inevitably disappears into the blending vats, some at least is turned into perfectly agreeable, fresh, simple whites of almost miraculous crispness given the warm climate.

Grapes with naturally high acidity are often a good bet for the production of champagne-method sparkling wine, where a thin, relatively neutral base wine gives the best results. In the Loire, there is, of course, Vouvray; Saumur is also a good source of such fizz, as is the wider regional appellation of Crémant de Loire.

Chenin Blanc (right) is a high-acid grape that favours the cooler climates of the Loire valley. Here, its acidity and susceptibility to botrytis are its keys to success, making fine sparkling wine and exquisite sweet wines that retain a thread of refreshing sharpness.

FRENCH ORIGINS

The central Loire valley - Anjou-Saumur and Touraine.

WHERE ELSE IS IT GROWN?

South Africa. Also California, Australia, New Zealand, and a little in Argentina.

TASTING NOTES

When young and dry, tart green apple and pear, occasionally something a little more exotic (passion fruit) in a good year. Mineral, even metallic, hardness on the palate, though often with paradoxical underlying hint of honey. Can have a dry nuttiness (walnuts) and an indeterminately damp smell, like old newspaper or wet woollens. Sweeter styles get progressively more honeyed without losing the tingly, appley acidity woven through them.

Loire

An unusually fine summer's day blazes down on the Chenin vines in the tiny AC of Bonnezeaux in Anjou (below), where some of the Loire's finest botrytised Chenins are produced.

Despite its appearance in many areas outside Europe, no region makes more of Chenin Blanc than does the Loire. It is the most important white grape variety in the two central parts of the valley - Anjou-Saumur to the west, and Touraine in the east.

In Anjou, particularly, cultivating Chenin is something of a challenge. So far north, the grape is a notoriously slow ripener and, as summers in these parts are not exactly torrid, a lot of Anjou Chenin is very acerbic and raw-tasting - not at all a style that would find many imitators beyond France's borders. Then again, that is exactly how the locals like it.

Autumns, though, are damp and warm enough to permit the regular development of the noble rot botrytis. It is in Anjou that the premier appellations for botrytised Chenin are found: Coteaux du Layon, which encircles the tiny and

very fine enclave of Bonnezeaux (an AC in its own right), and Quarts de Chaume. In the best years these wines are fully the equal of great Sauternes and Barsac because they have that nerve-centre of acidity that keeps them going into a well-balanced old age. Château du Breuil and Domaine de la Soucherie (Coteaux du Layon), Angeli (Bonnezeaux) and Baumard (Quarts de Chaume) are among the truly outstanding names.

The lesser-known appellation of Coteaux de l'Aubance makes some reasonably good, though much less rich, sweet wines.

In the west of Anjou is Savennières, the appellation that many consider to be the highest expression of dry Chenin anywhere in the wine world. In their first flush of youth, the wines make no concession to drinkability, tasting hard as nails and tightly clenched. Over maybe seven or eight years, they open out into an austere but profoundly beautiful maturity, full of minerals, bitter apples and bracing Atlantic fresh air. The word "racy" when applied to wine might have been coined just for Savennières. Domaine de la Bizolière, Baumard, and especially Joly at Coulée-de-Serrant (a single-ownership estate that has its own AC) are the names to conjure with.

Travelling eastwards into Saumur, we enter fizz territory. Sparkling Saumur is made by fer-menting the wine a second time in the bottle to produce carbon dioxide, exactly as in champ-agne. Made only, or almost entirely, from Chenin, it usually has quite a snap to it, and is dead dry. Gratien & Meyer make a very typical one.

In Touraine, the most important appellation of all for Chenin Blanc is Vouvray. Together with its lesser-known and less distinguished neigh-bour to the south, Montlouis, Vouvray puts the Chenin through its paces, making it dry, *demi-sec, moelleux*, botrytised and fizzy. Quality is highly variable, and the wines - as elsewhere - are very vintage-dependent, but when it shines, it really shines.

The best growers in Vouvray, whose wines constitute an invaluable introduction to this underestimated grape, are Poniatowski, Cham-palou, Fouquet's Domaine des Aubuisières, Château Gaudrelle and Huët. The last makes a superbly rich and complex sparkling Vouvray that is probably the finest French fizz outside the Champagne region.

Other Regions

SOUTH AFRICA

Chenin, or Steen as it is more often termed, is put to the same sort of versatile use in South Africa as it is in the Loire. It is even used in some of the monumental fortified wines for which the Cape was once justly famous.

The difference is that the drier styles don't tend to be that remarkable. There is no South African Savennières to help the grape shine. Occasionally, they can fill the mouth with a gum-cleansing feel that's like biting into a just-picked apple, but they don't seem to have the sharper aromatic definition produced by the cool northerly climate of the Loire.

Much better wines are made from nobly-rotted Chenin, when the flavours of tropical fruit, honey, bitter orange peel and barley-sugar all seem to mingle in some of the world's most diverting sweet wines. Fleur du Cap Noble Late Harvest is a good, and very fairly priced, example of this style. Nederburg Edelkeur is perhaps more complex, but at around twice the price.

AUSTRALIA AND NEW ZEALAND

Not many other non-European producers have taken Chenin seriously yet as the base for a varietal wine. There is a tendency to make it too rich for its own good. In Western Australia, a plump, oak-enriched example is made by Moondah Brook in the sweltering Swan Valley. The cooler climate of New Zealand is a more likely setting for successful Chenins, although Collards Chenin Blanc from New Zealand is similarly high in extract to the Moondah Brook.

CALIFORNIA

One or two California wineries have produced successful varietal dry Chenin, some of it oak-aged. Those from Folie-à-Deux in the Napa, and Hacienda in Sonoma, are both good, but the bulk of the Chenin crop elsewhere goes into everyday blended whites to give added acidity.

Chenin Blanc, or Steen vines on the Klein Constantia Estate, South Africa (above). Chenin has been the backbone of the country's white wine production.

Widely spaced Chenin Blanc vines in the Temecula valley, California (left), where the variety is still a minority taste.

GRENACHE

Established as a vital ingredient to spice up the famous wines of Rioja and Château-neuf-du-Pape, the much-travelled, overworked Grenache is quietly developing a fashionable status. Discerning winemakers have recognised its worth as a varietal.

SEASONED WINE experts may raise a collective eyebrow at finding Grenache has claimed a place in my pantheon of great grapes. It is extensively planted around the world, to be sure, far more than any other variety we have met so far, but just because of that much-travelled, overworked reputation it is normally only accorded a fairly lowly status in the wine-drinker's league table. I say it is time to update that view.

As befits a grape that has been around quite a while, Grenache can turn its hand to almost any style of red wine, from darkly brooding behemoths, thundering with tannin, through sleek, svelte, spicy young things, to light-footed strawberry numbers with more than a dab of sweet oak scent. It's also quite good at fruity rosé.

There is some dispute as to precisely where the grape originated but, despite its common name, it isn't a native of France. It came to southern France from Spain, which is still its most likely provenance and where it goes by the name of Garnacha. Its pre-eminent role, in both countries, is as a versatile mixer, but it possesses enough innate character to play the lead in many a red blend.

Two historically renowned wines - Rioja from Castile, and France's very first *appellation contrôlée*, Châteauneuf-du-Pape, in the southern Rhône - would be nothing without Grenache, and its influence extends way beyond the confines of those two areas.

In Spain, its principal blending partner is the celebrated home-grown variety, Tempranillo. Experiments with unblended Tempranillo have often foundered for lack of the spicy depth of flavour that Garnacha can impart. Not just Rioja, but its neighbour Navarra to the east, Penedés in Catalonia and the huge central Spanish plain of La Mancha all rely on Garnacha to greater or lesser degrees. In the currently fashionable Ribera del Duero, it makes cherry-fruited rosé (or, properly, *rosado*) wines.

Grenache made its way into southern France sometime after the 13th century, when the Aragon kingdom expanded into Roussillon over the Pyrenees. From there, it spread northeastwards into Languedoc and then to the southern part of the Rhône valley. As it travelled, Grenache found itself bedding down with traditional French grapes such as Syrah, Carignan, Cinsaut and Mourvèdre. That assemblage now represents the bedrock of red wines made anywhere from Côtes du Roussillon, up through Fitou, Corbières and Minervois, the pays de l'Hérault and into the Côtes du Rhône backwaters.

At its most exalted, Grenache plays an integral part in the Rhône appellations of Châteauneuf-du-Pape and Gigondas. Most Châteauneuf has more Grenache in it than anything else, and the sheer diversity of styles from one producer to the next indicates something of the grape's adaptability.

Not the least reason for its ubiquity in these southern vineyards is that it responds to torrid growing conditions where there is little rainfall. It ripens without fuss, and can effortlessly attain sufficient natural sugar to give high alcohol: 14 per cent is quite the norm in Gigondas. In particularly ripe vintages, it also exhibits more than a little of the black-pepper aromatics traditionally associated with Syrah.

Down in the southwest of the central-southern swathe of France known as the Midi, Grenache pulls off some extraordinary tricks in the *vins doux naturels* of Roussillon. Here it is made into a sweet red wine by essentially the same method as port - that is, stopping the fermentation halfway through by adding spirit. This incapacitates the yeasts and results in a strong, soupy red with some of its natural sugar left unfermented.

Rivesaltes, Maury and the coastal appellation of Banyuls are the key areas for these rather rare wines; Rasteau in the southern Rhône makes something similar.

Outside Europe, Grenache is rapidly gaining ground as a constituent of the Rhône-style blends attracting attention in California, and as a densely concentrated varietal wine in Australia.

Grenache (right) is a hardy vine that thrives in hot, dry conditions. It produces good alcohol and plenty of spicy, rich fruit that makes it the ideal backbone to many red blends.

ORIGINS
Almost certainly Spain. (A Sardinian theory has its adherents, mostly in Sardinia.)

WHERE ELSE IS IT GROWN?
Throughout the Midi, southern Rhône and Provence. California, Australia, northwest Africa.

TASTING NOTES
Usually marries a lightish red fruit - redcurrants, strawberries, raspberries, morello cherries - to a spiciness like black pepper or, quite often, ground ginger. Sometimes a floral violet-like note as well. In its fiercest manifestations in the hotter parts of Australia, it can be tarry, chocolatey, liquoricey, like the most concentrated Shiraz, often supported by a distinct sweetness, so that the wines imitate the structure of vintage port.

France

The typical stony soils of the southern Rhône (above). On such poor soils, Grenache can yield crimson-coloured reds with spicy depth of flavour.

In Châteauneuf-du-Pape (below) the "galets" - large stones - that cover the soil retain heat at night and encourage the Grenache to ripen fully.

Travelling southwards through France, you will find Grenache first raising its head in the southern stretches of the Rhône valley, south of the town of Montélimar. Although other grape varieties - Cinsaut, Mourvèdre, Carignan, as well as the Syrah of the northern Rhône - play significant parts in the blended red wines from here on down, Grenache is so often the dominant partner that anybody who develops a taste for these wines has by definition developed a taste for Grenache.

Châteauneuf-du-Pape, the most famous name around these parts, is a confusing appellation to understand as far as its red wines are concerned. The chances are that most commercial Châteauneuf is not really made in the style that the textbooks tell you to expect. Big and beefy, massively structured, with galumphing tannins to ensure long life - that's the theory. In fact, much of the wine is made in a considerably more delicate style than that, with gentle red fruit, satiny lightness of texture and minimal tannic extraction. As such, these are wines that can be drunk at two or three years old - far sooner than the northern Rhône reds - and can fall apart if kept too long.

Domaine Père Caboche offers a textbook example of the lighter, fruitier style. Those in search of the bigger style, full of meaty richness, should seek out the wines of Château

Rayas, Chante-Cigale, Château de Beaucastel, Château St-André or Domaine du Grand Tinel.

The wines of Gigondas to the northeast should satisfy the most diehard devotees of big and burly reds. They are almost invariably hugely alcoholic and rigid with tannin, and seem to demand the sort of ageing that Hermitage requires, although you won't find anything like the same amount of fruit. Domaine de St-Gayan and Château de Montmirail are the stars. The latter also makes fine Vacqueyras, a good appellation that is one of the newer southern Rhône ACs.

Lirac, on the opposite side of the river Rhône to Châteauneuf, is an unfairly overlooked appellation that offers some pedigree reds from the likes of Domaine les Garrigues. Just south of Lirac is Tavel, which makes rosé wines only, again predominantly Grenache. Don't think of these as frivolous pink sippers for summer; they are pale in colour (often the shade of a faintly yellowed onion-skin) and loaded with alcohol. They can also reputedly age well, if ten-year-old rosé is your bag.

The preponderance of southern Rhône production is accounted for by Côtes du Rhône, a catchall appellation that extends through the whole Rhône valley, from north to south. It may include Syrah-dominated reds from the north, like the celebrated bottling from Guigal, to inoffensive house-red styles from any number of small growers, négociants and co-operatives. Of the various satellite areas, Côtes du Ventoux is a more reliable proposition than Côtes du Rhône, with the wines of Jaboulet and La Vieille Ferme showing plenty of spicy complexity in most years.

In the Midi, Grenache dominates most of the traditional appellations. Corbières, Minervois, Fitou, Faugères - these were once bywords for rough-and-ready red slosh. The widespread improvements in winemaking technology (not all of them home-grown, it has to be said) have brought with them a consequent upswing in quality with the result that these wines, Corbières especially, are now rivalling the best of the Rhône for character and ageability.

La Voulte-Gasparets and Château Les Ollieux in Corbières, Ste-Eulalie in Minervois and Mont Tauch in Fitou are the names to convince the cynics.

Other Regions

SPAIN

Garnacha crops up all over the northern half of Spain and in the flat, arid centre. It is used to add depth to the more refined Tempranillo in the reds of Rioja and Navarra. In the large southeastern portion of Rioja known as the Rioja Baja, it is particularly widely grown, to the extent that some varietal Garnacha is bottled here. Rosados, the Spanish name for rosé wines, are usually likely to be partly or wholly Garnacha. Many can be rather rustic, but very young ones can possess an appealing strawberry freshness.

In the Catalan region of Penedés, the celebrated house of Torres makes a Garnacha-based red, Gran Sangredetoro, that is supple and rich, and usually has an appetising, slightly singed flavour, like spit-roasted meat. At the peak of achievement in Spanish Garnacha, though, sit the wines of Priorato, also in Catalonia but situated further west. These are densely textured, inky, fiery reds with colossal alcohol and structure (the regulations stipulate minimum alcohol of 13.75 per cent, higher than any other denominated table wine). If you're feeling brave, try the wines of Scala Dei.

AUSTRALIA

Talking of massively structured Grenache, some of Australia's growers are beginning to capitalise on the willingness of the grape to give big alcohol and strong colour in hot climates. They are making some of the most dramatic, muscle-bound reds the variety has yet produced. Rockford and Charles Melton in the Barossa produce some fine examples, the latter naming his Grenache-based blend "Nine Popes", in garbled homage to the name of Châteauneuf-du-Pape.

CALIFORNIA

The Rhône Rangers, that single-minded band of California growers inspired by the wines of the Rhône valley, have nearly all planted some Grenache, although as yet it is very much playing second fiddle to Syrah. The Bonny Doon winery in Santa Cruz has been the leading light in this movement: its Clos de Gilroy is a fine varietal Grenache, while British consumers have for some years been able to enjoy a special ultra-peppery cuvée of Grenache called The Catalyst. The ability of the grape to produce fine rosé wines is ably demonstrated by La Rosé Sauvage from the Edmunds St. John winery in Alameda, just inland from San Francisco Bay.

The hilltop town of Laguardia in Rioja (above), with the Sierra de Cantabria towering behind. Grenache is an important ingredient in the historic reds of Rioja.

The hot climate of South Australia's Barossa Valley (left) is ideal for producing some of the world's most powerful Grenaches. These vines were planted in 1936.

GEWURZTRAMINER

Unique among the white varieties, Gewürztraminer is very much a love-it-or-hate-it grape. Once tasted, never forgotten, its ostentatious, scented, rich character has made it the grape forever associated with Alsace.

WHETHER YOU enjoy it or not, your first taste of Gewürztraminer will certainly make an impression. While a simple Chardonnay may seem shy and retiring in the glass, Gewürz comes screaming out at you with some of the most unearthly and downright bizarre scents and flavours to be found anywhere in the world of wine. So strange can it taste that those encountering it unsuspectingly for the first time may wonder whether it has had some other flavouring added to it.

The parent variety seems to be of north Italian extraction, and was originally known simply as Traminer. Its highly scented offshoot, first identified in the 19th century, took its prefix from the German word for "spiced". By this time the grape had acquired, by natural mutation, a deep pink rather than green skin and had begun to yield an extraordinarily perfumed juice. Popular in Germany, Gewürz was widely planted in Alsace, which was part of Germany on and off for much of its history, though it is now of course incontrovertibly French.

Alsace is now its first home. While there are increasingly impressive examples being produced elsewhere, particularly in Germany, they never quite seem to attain the uninhibited aromatic splendour of the greatest Alsace wines. In an especially ripe year, it may combine musky fruit notes like lychee and squishy apricot, with ginger, cloves, talcum powder and a whole florist's shop of roses, violets and jasmine. It is usually pretty low in acidity, which makes it drinkable quite young, but roaring with alcohol, so that a little - combined with those unsubtle flavours - goes an exhaustingly long way.

Because of its larger-than-life character, Gewürz is constantly in danger of not being taken terribly seriously by those who are used to more restrained flavours in a white wine. In the long, dry summers of Alsace, it ripens to a tremendous richness, which accounts for all that alcohol, but even when fermented up to around

the 14-15 per cent levels I have seen on some, it still seems to retain a core of residual sugar that leads a lot of consumers to find it too sweet for a supposedly dry white wine.

Once the taste is acquired, however, it becomes clear that Gewürztraminer is without doubt one of the classic wine grapes. From a *grand cru* vineyard site owned by one of the top producers in Alsace, its peculiar intensity can be a mightily refreshing antidote to the container-loads of tell-'em-apart oaky Chardonnay that the wine market is awash with. The best Gewürzes will age, although they tend to be the ones that have unusually pronounced acidity to begin with, and there are not too many of these. You can bump up acid levels by picking the grapes earlier, but the less ripe they are, the less of that striking flavour you will obtain.

The dilemma over picking times is problem enough in Alsace. In warmer climates, it becomes a complete headache. Pick it too early, and you lose some of the flavour concentration that consumers expect to find in bottles labelled Gewürz; leave it too long, and it tastes unfocused and muddy. The difficulties of timing it right are largely why most efforts outside Alsace have so far failed to match the quality of the best wines produced in this little enclave of northeast France.

That said, some German growers are beginning to achieve convincing results with the variety, especially in the slightly warmer areas of the Pfalz and Baden. New Zealand is giving it its best shot, and there are isolated stars in South Africa and Chile.

For a grape that seems to be telling the winemaker that it wants to be sweet, it comes as no surprise to find that many Alsace and German growers make a late-picked Gewürz, delicately flowery Spätlese and Auslese in Germany, and peach-scented Vendange Tardive in Alsace. When conditions are right, the grape can acquire noble rot, and a wine with full-blown botrytis is termed Sélection de Grains Nobles in Alsace. These are massively dense, opulent dessert wines, tasting like orange and ginger marmalade - one of the great taste experiences.

The unmistakable livery of the Gewürztraminer grape (right). Unlike the green or golden colour of its fellow white grapes, Gewürz sports a dusky pink skin - a fitting outer expression of its flowery, highly perfumed character.

ORIGINS

For the Gewürztraminer specifically, possibly Alsace. For its less intoxicatingly scented forebear, Traminer, probably the south Tyrol area of northern Italy.

WHERE ELSE IS IT GROWN?

Apart from Alsace, it has important bases in Germany and Austria, less so in Spain and eastern Europe. Experimental plantings dotted around the southern hemisphere, and also the United States, particularly the Pacific Northwest.

TASTING NOTES

The list is well-nigh endless. Fruits are usually an eerily precise imitation of ripely juicy lychees, together with overripe peach or nectarine when the flesh is just starting to turn mushy. Some authorities dispute the spice connection evoked in the German word *Gewürz*, but there is nearly always a good sprinkling of ground ginger and often cinnamon, occasionally the scent of whole cloves and even a dusting of white pepper. Flowers are very much in evidence too - violets and rose-petals (often reminiscent of attar of roses, as in Turkish Delight) - and then there is a whole range of scented bathroom products - aromatic bath salts, perfumed soap, talcum powder. Gewürz from regions other than Alsace may present a toned-down version of all that, which may come as a relief to some.

Alsace

Gewurztraminer (spelt without the *umlaut* in Alsace) accounts for about a fifth of total vineyard plantings in Alsace. It is considered to be one of the golden four varieties (along with Riesling, Pinot Gris and Muscat) that may be planted in those areas designated the *grands crus*. Although Riesling is unofficially thought of as the first among this top division by the growers themselves, Gewurz is cherished for the forthright character that has made it the grape most ineradicably associated in consumers' minds with the region as a whole. Blowsy, spicy, exotic Gewurz just *is* the taste of Alsace.

The grape does exceptionally well on the often rather claggy, clay-based soils found in the Haut-Rhin area of Alsace. Its willingness to ripen well in the generally dry vintages of this very sheltered region allows its personality to shine through in the finished wine. In many ways, it is the antithesis in Alsace of the Riesling we looked at earlier, giving more alcohol

and less acidity, resulting in a considerably more forward style of wine.

Another quality that marks Gewurz wines out from their counterparts is their very deep colour. They usually have a richly burnished golden tone, not dissimilar to the most heavily oaked Chardonnays, a characteristic derived in their case not from the use of wooden barrels but from the distinctive pigmentation of the skin. Whereas most white grape varieties come in conventional shades of green, Gewurz, as befits its gaudy nature, is turned out in a deep pink livery that lends some of its blush to the wine itself. Sometimes you may imagine you can see a faintly pinkish tinge behind the deep yellow.

In the cooler years in Alsace, Gewurztraminer can seem a rather pale imitation of itself, both in terms of colour and flavours. Neither 1991 nor '93 were particularly good, for example, and the wine's resulting balance can be seriously skewed, so that you end up with something

The Clos Windsbuhl vineyard at Hunawihr, owned by Zind-Humbrecht (below). The Gewurztraminer from this site is one of the finest examples of what Alsace Gewurz can achieve.

thick and heavy, but without the depth of flavour to carry it off with any grace.

The classification of the theoretically better hillside sites in Alsace as *grands crus* began in the 1980s. While dogged inevitably by controversy over what should be included and what should not, it is clear that much of the land that has been incorporated is of sufficiently good quality to inspire the producers to their greatest efforts. Some of the best sites for Gewurztraminer are Brand, Goldert, Hengst, Kessler, Sporen, Steinert and Zotzenberg, but there are many more.

Wines with those names on the label are undoubtedly worth the extra cost over a bottle of basic Gewurz. Many producers are in the habit of labelling their wines Cuvée Réserve, supposedly indicating notably successful batches of a particular vintage, but as the term has no legal force, it has inevitably been abused by some, who get away with labelling their bottom-line productions as Réserve wines.

Co-operatives are an important part of the wine scene in Alsace, and vary enormously in quality. One of the most commercially significant, exporting substantial quantities, is also one of the most reliable - the Caves de Turckheim. Its Gewurztraminer from the Brand *grand cru* is generally intensely concentrated.

Any list of the greatest producers in Alsace invariably begins with Zind-Humbrecht. Its Gewurztraminers - especially the Herrenweg and Clos Windsbuhl bottlings, and some of the sweeter Vendange Tardive wines from *grand cru* sites like Hengst and Goldert - are unutterably exquisite, powerful essences of this most ostentatious grape.

Other good wines come from Hugel, Kuentz-Bas, Trimbach, Ostertag and Schlumberger.

Gewurztraminer grapes left on the vine until November, (above), destined for the peach-scented style of Alsace Vendange Tardive.

Other Regions

GERMANY

Although plantings of this grape in Germany are by no means extensive, some German growers have achieved notable successes with it in the light-textured, low-alcohol styles for which the country is renowned. It fares better in the warmer regions such as Baden, in the south, and the Pfalz, where its best exponent is the estate of Müller-Catoir, whose Gewürzes are full of expressive ripe fruit.

UNITED STATES

As others of the Alsace grape varieties, such as Riesling and Pinot Gris, have thrived in the states of the Pacific Northwest, so Gewürz has also done its bit. Success has come patchily and the results are not as yet much exported. In Washington State, Columbia Winery makes a reasonably tasty example, as does Kiona Winery with its late-harvest version.

NEW ZEALAND AND AUSTRALIA

The cooler climate of New Zealand is better for Gewürz than most of Australia, where the grape has often been used simply as blending material for dry Riesling. The North Island regions of Gisborne and Auckland have produced some convincing attempts, from wineries such as Villa Maria, Matua Valley and Morton Estate.

ELSEWHERE

Although "quiet" is the one epithet you don't expect to apply to this grape, the occasional quietly impressive Gewürz does crop up in other countries. There's Villiera from the South African region of Paarl, and Viña Casablanca from Chile. The Torres estate in Penedés in northeastern Spain successfully blends Gewürz with Muscat to make its Viña Esmeralda.

Matua Valley Winery, set amid its vineyards in the Auckland area of New Zealand's North Island (above). Matua Valley is one of New Zealand's most notable producers of characterful Gewürztraminer.

GAMAY

The one classic grape variety that has stayed close to home, Gamay is synonymous with Beaujolais, that light, fresh, strawberry-fruity red that is designed to be drunk young and lively.

LOOKING AT a map of the world distribution of grape varieties might seem to suggest that Gamay is something of an interloper among this exalted company of 12 noble grapes. A red blob shows a significant concentration of it in eastern France, with only the skimpiest of traces anywhere else. In fact, it gets in because that red blob constitutes one of the world's most individualistic red wine styles - Beaujolais.

Gamay is the only grape used in the making of (red) Beaujolais. Some is also grown further north, in the southern stretch of Burgundy known as the Mâconnais, where it is responsible for usually rather indifferent wines bottled as Mâcon Rouge. Elsewhere in Burgundy, it may be blended in a proportion of up to two-thirds with Pinot Noir to make Bourgogne Passetoutgrains. A fair bit is grown in the Loire valley to the west, some as Gamay de Touraine, some used in Crémant de Loire pink fizz. On the western flank of the central Rhône, in the Coteaux de l'Ardèche, it makes spicy reds to rival the Grenache-based wines of Côtes du Rhône.

It is on the stern, granite hillsides of Beaujolais, however, that the Gamay really comes into its own. In addition to basic Beaujolais and Beaujolais-Villages, there are ten villages that are theoretically capable of making the best wine (known as *cru* Beaujolais), and that are entitled to their own appellations within the region. Running north to south, these are: St-Amour, Juliénas, Chénas, Moulin-à-Vent, Fleurie, Chiroubles, Morgon, Régnié, Brouilly and Côte de Brouilly. The last is a peculiar little hill of blue granite that pops up in the middle of the larger Brouilly appellation.

There are some subtle stylistic differences among these ten, which we shall return to in the regional section on Beaujolais, but what links them is more important than what distinguishes them, and that is the sunny-natured Gamay grape. Gamay offers the lightest style of red

wine possible, full of simple strawberry fruit, fresh sappy acids and little or no tannin. It is meant to be drunk young and lively, not cellared for years like claret. Although the best growers do achieve a certain measure of complexity in their wines, and some of the best *cru* Beaujolais can age well for five or six years, most producers are content to turn out oceans of straightforward quaffing wine that reacts beautifully to chilling for summer drinking.

The light texture of Beaujolais derives from a method of vinification called carbonic maceration that is especially suited to the grape. Instead of pressing the berries in the normal way, which extracts some tannin from the skins and pips along with the juice, Gamay grapes are placed whole into fermenters from which the air has been driven out with carbon dioxide. The juice starts to ferment inside the whole grapes until the skins burst from the build-up of gas within them. The grapes at the bottom of the heap are crushed by the weight of those on top, and ferment in the normal way, but that is still gentler than pressing between metal plates.

Gamay's suitability for producing cheap, early-drinking, featherweight reds is what inspired the Beaujolais Nouveau race, which continues to this day. Those who feel like imbibing quantities of embryonic, just-fermented, acid-tingling red from the very latest vintage can indulge their passion freely in the third week of November.

There is a movement afoot in the region to introduce greater depth into the wines in an attempt to throw the happy-go-lucky, knock-it-back image of Beaujolais into some sort of relief. Some are using a proportion of normally fermented juice in order to introduce a little tannic kick; others are using new oak barrels in a region where such a thing was once anathema. Guy Depardon, in Fleurie, is an example of a producer swimming courageously against the tide. His top *cuvées* have the gingery, brambly concentration of northern Rhône Syrah.

External markets are still dominated by the wines of the powerful bulk producer Georges Duboeuf. For once, quantity does not preclude

Gamay (right) offers the lightest style of red wine, full of simple strawberry fruit, fresh, sappy acids and very little tannin.

quality because most of his wines are good. Much debate was occasioned, for example, when Régnié was promoted to become the newest *cru* in 1988, with many commentators wondering whether the region deserved its elevation. Duboeuf is producing about the only one worth drinking so far.

Switzerland uses Gamay extensively, often in blends with Pinot Noir, and there are some producers in California doing their best with it (J. Lohr's Wildflower Gamay is a reasonable approximation of the style of young *cru* Beaujolais.) By and large, however, Gamay doesn't perform well on different soils, and the style of wine it is happiest producing has not been a noticeably fashionable one for red wines in recent years, so there is not the incentive that there is with a variety like Pinot Noir to compete with the best of France.

Misty autumnal scene in Brouilly (left), one of the ten crus *of the Beaujolais region.*

FRENCH ORIGINS
Beaujolais.

WHERE ELSE IS IT GROWN?
Burgundy, Loire, Rhône. Switzerland and other central European countries. Minute amounts in California.

TASTING NOTES
At its deliriously ripest, fistfuls of pulpy wild strawberries. When very young (as Nouveau, particularly) it can have a synthetic smell like boiled sweets, reinforced by the crunchiness of its acidity in the mouth. That, and related aromas like peardrops, banana flavouring and bubblegum, are all fermentation smells accentuated by the fact that no air gets into it while it is vinifying. Some of the richer, meatier *cru* wines can take on the attributes of mature Pinot Noir after five or six years.

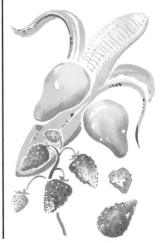

INDEX